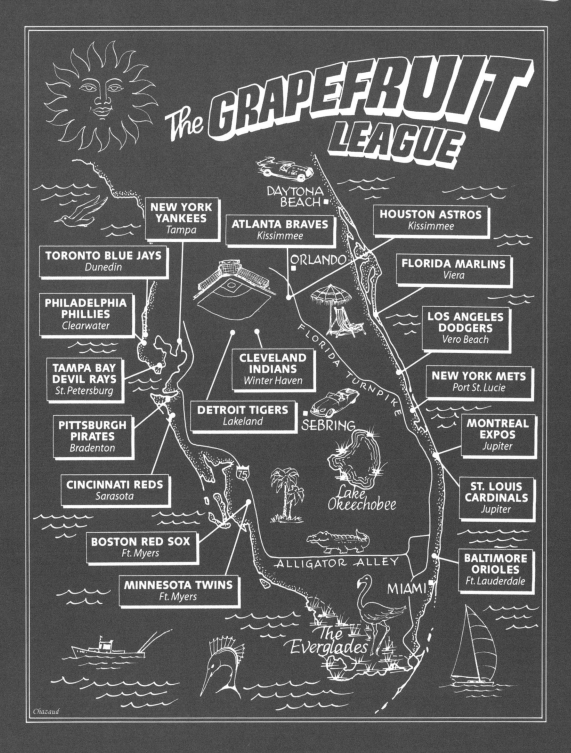

Baseball's Early Season

SPRING TRAINING

Baseball's Early Season

SPRING TRAINING

DAN SHAUGHNESSY AND STAN GROSSFELD

HOUGHTON MIFFLIN COMPANY

BOSTON NEW YORK

For Marilou and Stacey.

They know why.

Also by Dan Shaughnessy and Stan Grossfeld

Fenway: A Biography in Words and Pictures

For information about permission to reproduce selections from this book,
write to Permissions, Houghton Mifflin Company, 215 Park Avenue South, New York, New York 10003.

Visit our Web site: www.houghtonmifflinbooks.com.

Library of Congress Cataloging-in-Publication Data

Shaughnessy, Dan.
Spring training : baseball's early season / Dan Shaughnessy and Stan Grossfeld.
p. cm.

ISBN 0-618-21399-6
1. Spring training (baseball). I. Grossfeld, Stan. II. Title.

GV875.6 .S42 2003
796.357'64—dc21

2002027633

All photographs by Stan Grossfeld except:
Columbia Pictures: pp. 52-53; National Baseball Hall of Fame Library: pp. 48 (top), 48-49, 51, 55;
Ripken Baseball: pp. 18, 23; Sports Museum of New England (Laban Whitaker): p. 50;
Washington Post, © 1981 (Joseph Silverman, *Washington Star*): p. 16

Book design by Bill Marr, OpenBooks LLC
Maps by Jacques Chazaud
Printed in the United States of America
QWT 10 9 8 7 6 5 4 3 2

ST. PETERSBURG, FLORIDA

FORT MYERS, FLORIDA

TUCSON, ARIZONA

CLEARWATER, FLORIDA

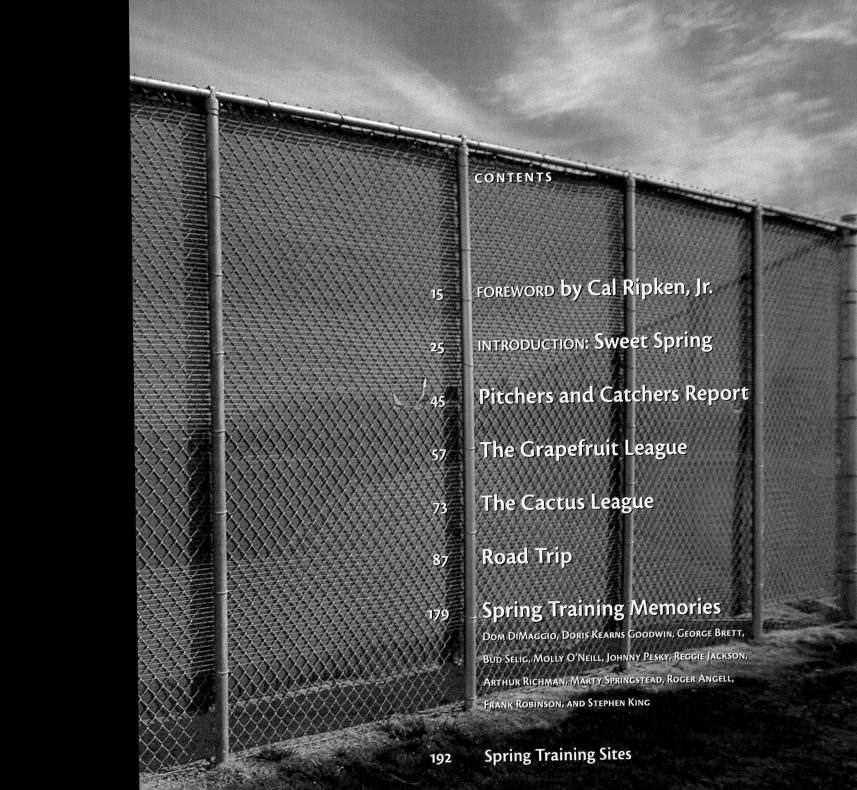

CONTENTS

FOREWORD

by Cal Ripken, Jr.

Cal Ripken, Jr., and Cal Ripken, Sr.,
Memorial Stadium

I think there's always a feeling of renewal in spring training, especially when you are coming out of a winter climate. You're thinking baseball. Spring. The weather's going to get warm. Everyone in the ball club is going to be happy to be back together as a group, happy just to be playing baseball again. It's simple, really. But then everything seems simpler when it comes to spring training. Even though you are still competing in an environment where people are watching you, you don't feel the same pressures that mount in the course of the regular season. You don't feel the weight of going to the big stadiums and playing the tough games. You don't have the road trips that take you too often away from home. You don't have to concern yourself with all the non-baseball issues that force you to take a more businesslike attitude when the games count, when everything you do counts. Of course you enjoy what you're doing during the regular season—I mean, it's playing baseball day and night, something nearly every one of us dreamed about—but in spring training there's a pure, unadulterated sense of just being able to play the game and have fun. Spring training is baseball the way it's supposed to be. It's exhibition mentality really. The games are more fan-friendly, more accessible. It's just a better people experience overall. For everyone—players, coaches, managers, writers, and certainly fans—spring training is a carefree, happy time.

For the players, there's even a certain giddiness when you first arrive at spring training. If I were driving to a site, I'd make sure to get there before the other team's batting practice started. It was a ritual. A lot of players tend to get to the ballpark earlier in the opening days. You'd waited all winter to see your teammates, the players from other teams too. You're just so happy to see everyone, you tend to overdo it. It usually takes a couple of days to settle in and get back to normal.

But as kids it didn't take us long to settle in. I was born in 1960, and by the time I was five or six, my dad's playing days were over, so we'd go to be with him for spring training. We'd go down during our spring break when we were in school—first to Thomasville, Georgia, then to Fernandina Beach, Florida. We'd stay at the hotel for the whole two weeks we were there.

There were four of us kids. My sister, Elly, is a year older than I am. Fred is a year younger, and Billy is four years younger than me. We drove everywhere at that time. Mom would pack up the car, a blue station wagon. We all jumped in and sang songs and looked at "South of the Border" signs all the way down from Maryland. I remember frequently having to pull over for pee stops. We would pick up those small Coke bottles at the gas stations, and occasionally, when the boys had to go to the bathroom, we'd actually use the Coke bottles so we wouldn't have to stop. I also remember sticking our heads out the window and having our hats sometimes blow off, and we'd have to stop and go back and scoop our hats up off the highway. Those were the good days—that pure feeling of spring and what it meant to feel alive.

Fernandina Beach stood out for me because I went into the locker room and couldn't get over all the bunk beds lined up in the complex where they had minor league spring training. They were army barrack–like beds, and I was fascinated by the notion of the players staying together every night and then going out together every day to play ball. Of course, several years later I was probably equally fascinated with the prospect of driving on the beach in Daytona when my dad trained there.

The Ripken clan: Cal Jr. is at left in the bottom row.

But as fun as it was for everyone, especially us kids, there was still a job to do—players to condition, rosters to write, plays to hatch, plans to make. In those days, my dad did whatever was needed. He wrote the whole program for Orioles spring training when he was in the minor leagues. I think he took the whole forty-five days and mapped it out, realizing that Rome wasn't built in a day. There was a process for spring training. When he was in the minors all those years, they ran his spring training program, so when he became the Oriole manager in 1987 and '88, he was running the spring program that he'd designed when I was a little kid.

Even as kids we had to fall in line too. We had a little time to mess around. But to be on the field, we had to be dressed in uniform. Nobody was allowed on the field without a uniform. They used to do sprints. I remember working on my crossover step, where they teach you how to run the lines. They let me run with the grownups. Those were *definitely* the days.

As we got older, spring training played a smaller part in our lives. We had school, so we'd only take short trips. We'd see Dad in spring training during our spring break, then join him in the summer wherever he was managing. But over the years we had quite a spring training run. Thomasville, Georgia, was first. Then Fernandina Beach. Then Daytona. Then Miami. When the Orioles moved their spring site to Miami, Dad actually participated in building the minor league complex. He hammered nails and poured concrete. It was Biscayne College then. Now it's St. Thomas of Villanova. We called it Iwo Jima.

In 1981 I finally came to spring training on my own terms. It was my first season in a big league camp as a player. Dad and I stayed in the Dupont Plaza Hotel in Miami that year. It was an unforgettable experience. Sure, I had grown up around baseball. I had witnessed it from the standpoints of both a fan and a kid—in many ways I had already lived it—but all of a sudden I was there because I had earned the right to be there as a player. I had made it to the big leagues, and this was my first real taste of just what that meant.

Miami Stadium was a field and a half. It was very efficient. The Orioles kept their numbers to a minimum there, and we got a lot of things done in a small area. I had played in the stadium in A-ball in the Florida State League in 1979, and I remember thinking how big that ballpark was. But when I returned for that first spring training in the big leagues, I realized it wasn't so big. I had developed into a better hitter with more power, and I got to thinking that that stadium was actually kind of small.

They played me a lot early that spring. I was so excited just to be wearing that big league uniform. Getting to play that much made it too good to be true. But as the spring went on, the regulars had to get ready for the season, and Doug DeCinces started to get more playing time in my place. When the first cuts came around, Earl Weaver called me into his office to break the news. I was on the first ship out of there, back to triple-A. Earl was an intimidating figure. We all knew he had a temper, and you didn't want to get on his bad side. I'd never been in his office alone. It was just the two of us, and he said, "You're not going to get at-bats. You really weren't going to make the team. We appreciate your effort. We like seeing you play. Now go down there and get your at-bats and get ready for your season."

I had hoped my dad would be the one to tell me, "Hey, you're going down." I hadn't known Earl very long, but Earl was good that way. It was his team, and he wanted to make sure that he was the one to deliver the message. After he told me, there was a dead silence, an intimidating silence, until I kind of squeaked out in my lowest voice, "Would it be okay if I hung around for the rest of the day and took a little extra batting practice?" He said, "Sure." So I went down to take batting practice. I wasn't too disappointed because I didn't expect to make that club. And I wanted to get used to big league facilities before I went back to the minor leagues. So I was swinging and hitting line drives. It was almost as if nothing had happened. But then a ball came inside on me a little quicker than I expected, and I popped on it and hurt my right shoulder. I knew something was really wrong.

Needless to say, when I went down after the cuts, I didn't play well at all. I rested a lot, and they weren't sure if I'd be able to start the season or not. A lot of people thought I had pulled an attitude muscle because I got sent down from the big leagues and hadn't come back to play. Still, I ran and did all the things to stay in shape. I just couldn't swing a bat because of the irritation it caused in my right shoulder. They wanted to put me on the disabled list, so I tested it out and didn't have any pain and I got a few hits before the spring was over and started the season very well. But I wonder what it would have been like if I hadn't pushed it and taken extra batting practice the day I got sent down.

The Orioles always stressed fundamentals at spring training. In Miami Stadium we had the "little field"—it was just a half-diamond for your stations and fundamentals. You'd work on your rundown plays and pickoff plays. We separated people into different groups and went about our work systematically. You had to be organized and efficient to get the best use out of that little field. It was just down the third base line, and we didn't have the protection from batting practice that we should have had. There was no net or anything, so extra people had to stand guard while we worked our stations. There were guards outside, too. It was normal to have our clubhouse broken into. Gloves and equipment were stolen all the time. Brooks Carey, my first roommate in my first big camp, brought his girlfriend down to spring training. She was at our game in Miami and went to the bathroom, where she was punched and mugged. Now it's almost impossible to imagine that these things could happen during spring training.

It's certainly a time when everything seems fresh and new. Spring training always reminds me of my first stolen base in the big leagues. It came from one of those plays we worked on every spring on the little field. The play is run when you have runners on first and third, there's a left-handed pitcher on the mound, and normally you run it with two outs and a two-strike count on the hitter. You watch the pitcher early in the count because you might put the play on. You see what his head action is. If he takes a look at the guy on third and then looks at the guy on first, the idea is this: as soon as the guy takes his head off you at third, the guy on third breaks first. He runs at a dead sprint. Then the guy on first reacts to the guy who runs, and he can either start running or fall down. When you move, you are right in the pitcher's face, so if he reacts in the slightest way toward first, it's too late to get the guy going home from third.

That's how I got my first steal in the big leagues. Jon Matlack was on the mound. It was one of those moments where you are taking a risk if you are on the bases. Under Earl Weaver, not too many people were allowed to take risks, let alone be on your own. His philosophy was to make out at the plate, not on the bases. So when he put that play on all of a sudden, I couldn't help but get excited. You hardly ever get a chance to make a play like that. The signal was two hands around the belt. But you would have communication with the first base coach and the third base coach. You were looking for that. So the play was on. I was on third and watching Matlack closely to make sure he was doing the same thing the same way every time. As soon as he took his head off me, I took off in a dead sprint. Matlack stepped off the mound and looked for a split second to the first base side. It was working. He didn't realize what was happening behind him. He threw a snap throw to the plate and the catcher caught it, but I beat the throw. It was a beauty of a stolen base. Later, we tried to run that play a couple of times in Yankee Stadium, but Donnie Mattingly was the only one who really understood it. He would see it brewing and come in and warn the pitcher. I was on third and Eddie Murray was on first and we got caught in a major rundown, though we got back safely. Overall, I think I was only involved in that play, for real, about three times. And for that I felt fortunate. Really, that kind of play is pure spring training. You might pull it off only once or twice a summer, once or twice a career even, but you still have to know how to do it. And spring training was always the place to get it down.

In those days there was a lot of continuity between the minor leagues and the big leagues, so it wasn't necessary to teach the play and go over it again and again. We'd run it a few

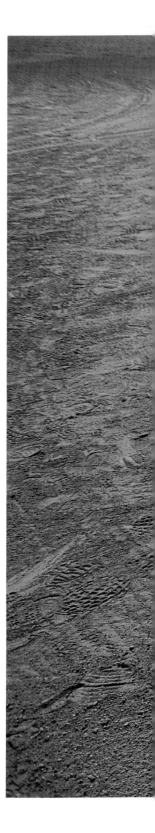

SPRING TRAINING

times in spring training, maybe two or three, but it was all just a refresher course. That continuity had the same impact on all the drills we did. The preparation was just more streamlined when you were hearing the same thing in the majors that you had heard in the minors. Success had everything to do with continuity within an organization. And the Orioles at that time were a model organization in that regard. Fundamentals were ingrained in you from the start. The accumulation of those same fundamentals over the years was vital. So when you got to spring training, these things weren't lofty, unattainable goals. They were simply a continuation of that deeper base knowledge you'd been acquiring for years.

Nowadays, you bring people into spring training and you have to start by teaching the fundamentals, so there's not time to grasp as much, certainly not the finer points or the special plays. You realize that execution and the ability to understand a play require more than a little refresher course. It takes *years* to perfect. But then it takes years for a player to come into his own and perfect his game. Starting over every spring can make that mountain seem an impossible climb.

I used to see people who would do nothing in the off-season and then come to spring training, only to get hurt in the first week. Me? I just like to stay in shape—baseball or not. I like to stay active, so basketball's my off-season game. I could never understand why someone would risk coming to spring training out of shape. And it was a risk. So, almost from the start, I decided that I was going to stay in shape all year long so that when spring training rolled around, I could use it for what it's supposed to be—we sometimes lose sight of it—and that's getting ready for baseball. Of course there's a difference between being in good shape and being in good baseball shape. The latter is hard to maintain during the off-season when you live in a colder climate. The truth is that there's only so far you can throw and so much you can hit when the temperature is your biggest opponent.

Early in my career, I'd come out of those cold temperatures anxious to get started playing baseball again. I thought the more at-bats I got in spring training, the more ready I would be for the regular season. But as I got older, I realized that that wasn't true. You really need a specific number of at-bats—not too many, not too few. Ideally, you want to work through spring training so that when Opening Day arrives, you are at your peak. You don't want to take too many at-bats and then peak with two weeks to go before the regular season. You risk starting that downhill slide we've all suffered through.

Results in spring training don't matter. In fact, looking back on my career, I realize that some of my greatest spring trainings, power-wise, didn't equal a good month of April. And after some of my worst spring trainings, I had the best starts of my career. So there never seemed to be a direct correlation. And that's because spring training is just about getting ready, *knowing* that you're ready, and of course coming out of it all injury-free.

Spring training was never just about the play on the field, though. There were the bus rides to the games. No spring training experience is complete without a trip across Alligator Alley. I remember Earl Weaver's philosophy about taking all his guys on the road. He felt a responsibility to have his key players at all the games. We didn't play the whole game, but we would take our show on the road and get one or two at-bats. As we got older, though, different managers had different philosophies. Some wanted to protect their players from the rigors of travel. I would always go in and discuss it with the manager. They would ask me how I saw spring training. They would ask for a guideline. Myself, I always felt obligated not to miss the same city two games in a row. So I never molded my spring training on the duration of those long, dusty bus rides.

Of course, that trip from Miami to Fort Myers across Alligator Alley strained my resolve. It made for a long day. And that ballpark was hot. I always thought Alligator Alley was a myth. It became a running joke. Someone would yell, "Gator on the right." And we'd whip our necks around, never to see a gator. But once you did, you knew what to look for—a log floating on the water. Soon you're the one yelling, "Gator on the right," and you mean it. I know guys who never laid eyes on one—at least they didn't know it. But as sure as I'm Cal Ripken, Jr., there were gators on that drive.

We used to make a team trip up to the west coast, but there were enough teams in South Florida, so we could generally keep our trips to a minimum. The best was going to play the Yankees in Fort Lauderdale. There was always a certain excitement there, a sense of history about the players who had played on that field. We played a lot of games there over the years, but I'll never forget one night when it was raining hard and the game should have been canceled. Instead, George Steinbrenner had them light the infield on fire to dry it, and then they brought in helicopters, their blades beating low to the ground, to help dry out the field. Talk about a rain delay. Those things don't happen anymore.

For anyone in or around baseball and for any fan, spring training becomes a kind of annual ritual, a time when the baseball year comes full circle. It's the moment a new cycle begins. Before long, it was my kids coming to see me at spring training, just as we had visited my dad all those years ago. Before they started school, my kids were with me for the whole time, and then, when school intervened, they were just with me for spring training. But we would cheat a little, take them out early, return them late. It was important for the family to be together. They were as much a part of my spring training as hitting and throwing were. They were fundamentals, to be sure.

But as much as the ritual of spring training seems to have stood the test of time, the business of spring training has certainly evolved. New ballparks have been built; the atmosphere has changed. When you look back at those old ballparks—Miami Stadium, Pompano, Fort Lauderdale, Old West Palm Beach—you realize just how special that throwback character is, that classic feel. They make you think of baseball in a very elementary way. Now you have the newer spring training complexes, with multiple fields that allow you to do more things. They are needed for functional teaching and training, but no matter how nice they are, they aren't half as charming. Now more and more people are coming, and you lose the intimacy that spring training used to have. These days it sometimes seems like you're running a hundred players through a drill.

Hey, things change. There are a lot of things that are different about spring training—things I miss, things I don't, things that affect to various degrees the fans' enjoyment of this great game. But all in all, spring training is still a good, fun experience, a moment in baseball time to be savored. I know it's given me some of my favorite memories, both on the field and off.

— CAL RIPKEN, JR.
Baltimore, Maryland

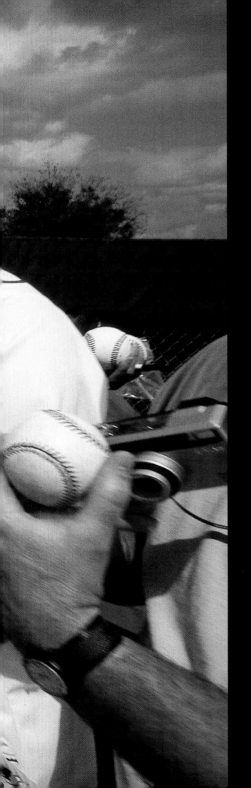

SWEET SPRING

Baseball's Early Season

Before the purpose-pitch that zips inches from the batter's head, before green-fly autograph seekers stalk hotel lobbies, before hateful sports talk radio jockeys spill their venom, before thousands of fans stand up and boo in 50,000-seat stadiums, before the proverbial dog days of summer and the pressure-packed moments of October . . .

There is sweet spring. The long hello. Baseball's early season.

Spring training. It's a simple, two-word phrase with connotations guaranteed to lift the spirits of anyone who loves baseball. Spring training means renewal. It is baseball's new year. Just as Roman Catholics purge their sins with confession and contrition, baseball players report to Florida and Arizona with clean slates, full of infinite hope and potential. Pitchers are 0–0 with ERAs of 0.00. Hitters have zero strikeouts and no runners left in scoring position. Thirty major league teams are undefeated, all tied for first place. Back in the frozen North, energetic and innocent fans think maybe this will be the year for the woebegone Kansas City Royals, Detroit Tigers, or Pittsburgh Pirates. It's okay to dream in February. Some teams are never as good as they are before the games actually start.

Other professional sports have nothing similar. Football, basketball, and hockey have exhibition seasons, tuneups that they insist be called "preseasons." In truth, these are merely conditioning-attrition boot camps, usually held near the city where the team plays its home games during the regular season. There is nothing remotely quaint or remote about any of it. The self-important National Football League presents the worst of American sports preseasons. It's the ultimate sports meat market. Sadistic coaches run dozens of players through two-a-day drills in Savannah summer heat, which induces cramping, vomiting, and dehydration. Occasionally a player dies from the workouts. Offensive tackle Korey Stringer died of heatstroke at the Minnesota Vikings' August training camp in

DAVENPORT, FLORIDA

JUPITER, FLORIDA

Mankato, Minnesota, in the summer of 2001. He vomited three times in practice, and his body temperature was 108 degrees when he was admitted to the hospital. Only the strongest and fittest NFL mastodons survive to play in the four phony preseason games, which bloated NFL owners make part of their season-ticket packages. Charging full fare for NFL preseason ball is true consumer fraud.

Where football's early season is controversial, hockey's and basketball's preseasons are entirely forgettable, lacking all form of ritual and tradition. Teams train in relative secrecy, staying close to home unless some inventive soul like Pat Riley chooses a tropical outpost to condition his Lakers, Knicks, or Heat. Fringe players are run in and out of camp like so much human chattel, and only the most devout fans pay mind to early cuts and game results. Newspaper and broadcast coverage is relatively light, especially since these sports hold their preseason camps during the height of baseball's pennant races and football's season launch.

Contrast all of the above with baseball's spring training. Hardball's early season is a six-week, laid-back warmup followed by legions of retirees and vacationers, many of whom wait to inspect Grapefruit and Cactus schedules before they plan their February-March trips. My personal favorite moment of each spring comes after the first full-team meeting, when the team takes one lap around the warning track before the players commence with stretching and drills. That's right—one grueling lap. It's a great juxtaposition to the preseason drills of football, basketball, and hockey.

Legitimate year-round conditioning by most modern baseball players has rendered much of spring training obsolete, but few are calling for the early season to be shortened. In fact, the baseball boom of the last twenty years (too often interrupted by those nasty work stop-

WINTER HAVEN, FLORIDA

pages) has transformed spring training into a cottage industry for franchise owners. In 2002 the *Wall Street Journal* reported that spring training had an economic impact of $600 million. Preseason ticket sales were running 20 percent higher than in 2001. In an average spring, more people attend spring training games than attended NFL games over a five-year period. Of thirty big league baseball teams, twenty sell a higher percentage of their ticket inventory in spring training than during the regular season.

The surge in spring training's popularity is not an entirely positive development. The average spring crowd is only 6,000 fans, and the entire spring season draws a little over 2.5 million fans, but it's become difficult to score tickets in too many spring sites. In places like Tampa (Yankees), Fort Myers (Red Sox), Kissimmee (Braves), and Peoria, Arizona (Mariners), this loss of the spontaneous ticket purchase has sucked some of the charm from the spring season.

Still, spring provides relief from a winter of hardball money news. Free agent signings can be exciting, but too much of the November–January baseball reportage concerns labor, arbitration, ballplayer relocation, trade speculation, and all other forms of player transaction. The hot stove season keeps the fires burning, but too much of it is muddied by money and litigation.

Then comes the fresh air of spring, a time to see the pro game up close, in beautiful slow motion, removed from the madness that too often marks regular-season play in all four major professional leagues. There are still sites in Bradenton, Florida (Pirates), and Phoenix (A's) where routines of the past are not yet tainted by the commercialization and exploitation of modern times. Spring training is an acoustic James Taylor ballad in a world of Metallica. Wooden music beats heavy metal anytime.

"Spring training is one of the few things that's remained fairly constant in our game," said Commissioner Bud Selig. "The game has changed so dramatically in so many ways, but not spring training. It's just the most wonderful time of the year."

Cubs general manager Andy MacPhail, a baseball lifer whose father and grandfather are both enshrined in Cooperstown, added, "I've been going since I was nine years old. The thing that strikes me now is how much more popular the games are. When I was a kid, a good spring crowd was 2,000 people. Today we can draw 10,000–12,000 fans. It's grown, and it means so much to the economies of the cities we play in. I look at how the stadiums and facilities have improved and how many people are trying to reach back to baseball when it was a simpler, less complex game. I think there's an appeal to the game of baseball that has increased over the last couple of decades. Sometimes the more complex our society becomes, the more people are reaching for what was once described as a pastoral lawn game, which is what baseball is."

Spring training is certainly a lot cheaper than anything you'll find during the regular season. Most teams sell lawn seats for as little as five bucks. Parking, too, is almost always five dollars. Imagine. You might get to recline on the grassy knoll behind the outfield fence, drinking beer, waiting for homers. You won't wait for much else. Most parks are overrun with volunteers and concessionaires. It sometimes seems as if every fan has his own personal vendor. And even if you do have to wait here, it's always a pleasure, part of the experience.

But then, more than any game, baseball is about anticipation. Players know. Fans know. Appreciation comes from attentiveness to what *might* happen. Watching the non-action before it unfolds can be as much fun as seeing what transpires when the ball is actually hit and runners start going around the bases.

True seamheads are trained to be suspicious of those who believe baseball is too slow. It's *supposed* to be slow. That's the point. Don't trust those who tell you they hate baseball because it's slow. It's important to spot this character flaw. People who prefer "action" sports— linear games, governed by clocks, with steady progressions to the goal—are more likely to be shallow. Deep thinkers are better able to appreciate baseball, and it is this level of thought that plays to the beauty of spring training. The anticipation is often better than the actual.

Nothing in pro sports is more steeped in anticipation than baseball's spring season. It is believed that the expression "Hope springs eternal" was coined sometime early in the twentieth century by a baseball scribe on the take, eating free food and drinking the ball club's booze while staying in a luxury St. Petersburg hotel room supplied by the ball club he was covering.

Predictability is one of the odd comforts of spring training. There are annual stories that make the world right for longtime baseball fans. No self-respecting major league spring camp would be complete without at least one star veteran who arrives late, plus the obligatory Latin American ballplayer who is detained because of visa problems. Baseball writers have a handy index of well-worn spring themes, and these topics rank right up there with the unwashed phenom (Clint Hurdle on the cover of *Sports Illustrated* in 1978), the overweight veteran (Britt Burns in Yankee camp in 1986), the contract holdout (Tris Speaker in 1911, Don Drysdale and Sandy Koufax in 1966), the manager on the hot seat (John McNamara in 1988), the fading old-timer who announces that he is in the best shape of his career (Bob Stanley, almost every year), and the late spring release of a onetime highly paid star (Jose Canseco, cut by the Expos in 2002).

TAMPA, FLORIDA

SPRING TRAINING

Historically, racetracks, card games, and hotel bars have been rough on spring training. Ball club owners in the old days liked to think of spring as a time for players to dry out, but drinking generally increased once the fellows reunited at training camp. Money changed hands regularly at poker games, and spring training has been a friend of Florida racetracks for more than a century. Don Zimmer, a baseball lifer for more than a half century, stalks the tracks wherever he goes, and Yankee manager Joe Torre happily rides sidecar with him. Even the scribes get involved. A reporter covering a team in Jupiter, Florida, in the spring of 2002 made $45,000 in a single night at the racetrack.

More than anything else, spring training promotes hope and inspires action at the box office. This is what keeps spring training going for six long weeks. Pitchers take longer than hitters to get their arms ready for the big league season, but in this age of huge money and year-round conditioning, players no longer need a month and a half to prepare.

PORT ST. LUCIE, FLORIDA

"It could be two weeks shorter," said Seattle manager Lou Piniella. "The pitchers might need a little more time, but these players are ready after a couple of weeks."

Before free agency, many baseball players got real jobs during the off-season. In mid-December, you could bump into your team's relief pitcher selling fishing rods on the floor of a Sears department store. Players who didn't get jobs usually ate themselves out of shape (or added fifteen pounds giving speeches-for-hire on the rubber chicken circuit). These players would show up in Florida and Arizona and run themselves back into condition. That could take six weeks. "We used spring training to get in shape," said Yogi Berra. "That's a big change. We had to go to work in the off-season, so we didn't stay in good shape for baseball."

Just as ballplayers don't take the train to spring training and don't hike through the woods anymore, they also no longer work in the off-season. There's too much money to be made just by staying in the big leagues, so you'd better be in shape when you arrive at spring training or some young stud will have your job. Today's players have the incentive and the equipment to stay buff year-round. Only a foolish major leaguer lets himself go during the four months between seasons.

The spring of 1990 proved that it doesn't take six weeks for big leaguers to get ready for baseball. A labor dispute caused baseball to hold a hurry-up spring of only three weeks. No problem. When the regular season started, the games showed no depreciation in play. After the strike of 1994, which wiped out the 1994 World Series, owners went with "replacement players" during spring training and threatened to play a charade of a regular season with the misfits who'd crossed the lines of the Major League Players Association. The strike ended on the eve of Opening Day, and baseball called for another abbreviated spring season to prepare for a return to the field. After twenty days of spring training, the season started. Again, there was no measurable loss in the quality of play.

Spring training is when the eager young players overachieve and when some of the grizzled vets go through the motions. Joe Black, the first black pitcher to win a World Series game and who passed away just shortly after spring training in 2002, remembered when he was a kid, pitching to a veteran Hall of Fame slugger who went by the name of "the Kid": "It was my first year with the Dodgers, and we played exhibition games in Miami. That's the first time I ever saw Ted Williams. It was 1952. Jimmy Piersall came up first, then Harry Agganis, then Bobby

SCOTTSDALE, ARIZONA

Doerr. I'd heard all this about Ted Williams and I was out there pitching to him. He hit me hard, a double against the wall. He trotted into second base and said, 'Hey, come here.' I walked halfway out there and he said, 'You're gonna be a helluva pitcher.' I said, 'Well, you just hit my fastball.' He said, 'Everybody's not Ted Williams!'"

The *New Yorker*'s Roger Angell, one of the first to chronicle the charms of spring training, wrote, "Players are what you go to watch in the spring; teams don't begin to emerge until summer." In this spirit, nothing is more meaningless than spring training standings. There is a mountain of evidence to support this. Spring training champs annually finish in the basement during the regular season, and it's not unusual for World Series winners to look back at the Grapefruit or Cactus standings and recall the 10–20 spring record. The 2001 Seattle Mariners went 13–19–1 in spring training, then won a major league record-tying 116 regular-season games. The Yankees won back-to-back World Series in 1999 and 2000 despite an aggregate spring record of 27–39 in those two years.

Other than baseball, food is the dominant topic in the Florida and Arizona camps. Restaurant talk is the backbeat of almost every spring training conversation. *How was the veal? Did you have to wait for a table? Pricey, wasn't it? Was the service okay?* It is the conversation starter in the hotels, in the stands, and around the batting cages. Former Orioles trainer Ralph Salvon was famous for talking about his next meal while devouring the one in front of him. Salvon and Jim Palmer annually drove from Baltimore to spring training, and Palmer referred to the trip as "an eleven-hundred-mile smorgasbord."

There are wonderful individuals in this world who consider a baseball box score one of the four major food groups—something to be devoured during breakfast along with eggs, toast, and ham. The first spring box in the morning paper provides sustenance for hungry hardball addicts who've been starving since late October. It matters not that those early spring boxes are filled with the names of has-beens and never-will-bes. The first spring box score of 1919 involved the defending World Champion Boston Red Sox and the New York Giants. Most of the Sox made the trip on a coastal steamer that sailed from New York. Boston's star pitcher, Babe Ruth, wasn't on the boat because he was embroiled in a contract dispute with owner

FORT LAUDERDALE, FLORIDA

Harry Frazee. Ruth was threatening to leave baseball and become a professional boxer, claiming he had a $5,000 offer to fight a heavyweight contender named Gunboat Smith. (In 1978, future Brewer Hall of Famer Robin Yount briefly threatened to switch to pro golf.)

Ruth eventually came to terms with Frazee, and in the Sox first spring game at the Tampa Fairgrounds, on April 14, 1919 (postwar complications delayed spring training), Ruth batted against Giants pitcher "Columbia" George Smith and hit a home run that traveled between 500 and 600 feet. The successful southpaw hurler had already hit twenty big league homers, but many believe that it was his blast in Tampa that made him an everyday player for good.

The longest home run (preseason, regular season, postseason inclusive) these eyes have seen in forty-nine years would be a shot hit by Bo Jackson off Dennis "Oil Can" Boyd in Davenport, Florida, near the intersection of Routes I-4 and U.S. 27. Driving west on I-4 after landing at the Orlando airport, I never fail to recall this homer when passing the site of the old Kansas City Royals spring complex. Subsequent conversations revealed that the Can told Bo before the game that he was going to challenge him with a fastball down the middle. Clearly, Bo accepted the challenge and made some Florida history with his Baseball City bomb. It traveled over a monstrous 71-foot left-center field scoreboard and landed in a cow pasture beyond the fence.

The intrepid Angell has an even better story about a spring training blast. In March of 1975, Angell watched the Mets play the Yankees at Fort Lauderdale Stadium (then the spring home of the Yanks, now the Orioles) and saw Dave Kingman launch a rocket off a pitch from Catfish Hunter. As Angell recalls, it was an offspeed pitch, and Kingman hit it over a left field fence, "about three palm trees high," onto an adjoining ball field at Lauderdale. Mickey Mantle, no stranger to tape-measure shots, was coaching for the Yankees that day and said it was the longest homer he'd ever seen. Yankee manager Bill Virdon, noting the diamond beyond the fence, said that it was a homer on one field and a double next door. Recalls Angell, "Kidding Catfish afterward, Kingman really relished it. He teased, 'Wait till the regular season, you're really gonna see something.'"

Rarely is there any hooting or discouragement from the stands at spring training. Most spring games are played in towns populated by older, retired Americans. Toss in the devout legions who fly south and west to see their favorite teams and you have a unanimously supportive fan base. It's almost impossible for a player to get booed during spring training. The blue-hairs aren't likely to curse players, and fans who save vacation time for spring training generally want only positive news. It's the same in the parking lots outside the ballparks and in beer lines under the stands: you will not find a happier crowd at a professional sporting event.

Flag-wavers make spring training special. Flag-wavers are the elderly zealots who hold orange flags and direct cars into the parking lots before a game. In most cities they are volunteers, happy just to be a part of the spring training experience. They hold flag-waving seminars during the winter to prepare for the upcoming season. The object is to get the maximum number of cars into small lots (usually unpaved acres) in as orderly a fashion as possible. They take their job seriously. Woe is the "I'm late, I'm important, and I'm in a hurry" northeasterner who crosses paths with a Kissimmee flag-waver.

With a pace like this, it's no wonder that spring training seems perfectly designed for the elderly. Fear not if you are driving to a game in St. Petersburg and find yourself following

TAMPA, FLORIDA

what appears to be a driverless automobile. It's not Roland-the-Headless-Thompson-Gunner. It's just another shrunken senior, barely able to see over the steering wheel. In some spring training parking lots, it seems as if the handicapped spaces outnumber the rest.

This is big league ball without the moat. Fans at the spring sites are far more likely to encounter their heroes doing everyday chores. You might run into Ken Griffey, Jr., at the Winn Dixie in Sarasota, Florida. Find the Cubs team hotel in Mesa, and you might see Tom Gordon hanging around the pool after finishing his morning workout. Is that Tom Glavine up ahead at the miniature golf course? No one is in a hurry. Ballplayers and fans share the sense that there is nowhere else to be and nothing else to do.

Spring training is where Oriole Curt Blefary made his teammates drive 80 miles north of Miami to get great ice cream, then ordered vanilla. It's where an eighteen-year-old Robin Yount sat on a bus from Sun City to Mesa and was told by manager Del Crandell that he'd be going to Milwaukee as the starting Brewers shortstop. It's where Ted Williams and Carl Yastrzemski played tennis against each other at a Winter Haven Ramada Inn in 1979.

It's where Bill Clinton spoke with Wade Boggs outside the dugout at the Astros complex in Kissimmee, Florida, during the early stages of his 1992 campaign (both Clinton and Boggs had mistress problems before it was over). It's where historian Doris Kearns Goodwin played catch with her young sons in the quad of the Winter Haven Holiday Inn. It's where Twins owner Calvin Griffith stood on the balcony of his Orlando condo and stared blankly into the sky at the wreckage of the *Challenger* spacecraft. It's where ballplayers annually organize an NCAA basketball pool for March Madness. It's where fans tailgate in the parking lots outside

KISSIMMEE, FLORIDA

HoHoKum Stadium when the Cubs welcome the Giants to Mesa.

It's where young shortstop John Valentin criticized the infield at the new ballpark in Fort Myers, only to get ripped in the papers by the mayor. (Did Richard Daley ever rip Ernie Banks?) It's where the Yankee brain trust went to the George Steinbrenner Room of Malio's restaurant in Tampa to hatch the trade that would bring Roger Clemens to New York. Malio's has a Steinbrenner Room and a Lou Piniella Room. The Steinbrenner Room has a private telephone for George.

Spring training is where an angry Clemens stormed out of camp in Winter Haven in 1987, prompting Red Sox general manager Lou Gorman to say "The sun will rise, the sun will set, and I'll have lunch." It's where Yankee outfielder Ruben Rivera was cut loose after he stole a glove from the locker of Derek Jeter, then sold it to a collector for $2,500. Rivera was immediately dubbed "the New Yankee Clipper."

It's where Arizona Diamondback manager Bob Brenley pinch-hit for his pitcher in the bottom of the eighth of a 2002 Cactus League game against the White Sox, then put the hurler back in the game to pitch the top of the ninth. Brenley checked with the ump. He checked with Chicago manager Jerry Manuel. No problem. It's only spring training.

The Yankees were enjoying an otherwise calm spring training in 1973 when pitchers Fritz Peterson and Mike Kekich announced that they were swapping wives, kids, and houses. Yankee general manager Lee MacPhail said, "We may have to call off Family Day."

Spring training is where Cy Young was excused for a couple of weeks because he had a job tutoring pitchers at Harvard University. It's where eighty-two-year-old Red Sox lifer Johnny

TEMPE, ARIZONA

"My first camp was in 1977. I was number 69—it went in alphabetical order."

—Alan Trammel

Pesky resumes chomping on chewing tobacco. A veteran of sixty spring trainings, Pesky waits until late February to break out the chew, and he can tell stories of riding on barnstorming trains with Jimmie Foxx and having Foxx boost him into the upper bunk of a sleeper.

Spring training is where when the Twins play home games at Lee County Stadium in Fort Myers, public address announcer Bob Casey never fails to bellow "Temperature at game-time, 84 degrees. Temperature in Minneapolis, 4 degrees!"

And the cornball crowd always roars.

Spring training is where you see pitchers running in the outfield on the warning track while the game is in progress. It's where some of those pitchers wear numbers like 89 and 95. It's where the Cincinnati Reds in 2002 sent a batter to home plate wearing a uniform jersey with no name and no number (see page 36). It's where major league players file off a bus in full uniform, like high school kids arriving to play a league rival.

It's where scouts sit behind the backstop, wearing straw hats, holding radar guns, and charting the miles-per-hour of pitches thrown by a young man who might look good in some-body else's uniform someday soon. Spring training is where frontline players usually leave the game after five, four, or even three innings to go fishing. The managers of visiting teams are required to bring only a handful of starters. When the Cincinnati Reds take a bus from Sarasota to Clearwater, Ken Griffey, Jr., sometimes has the option. You don't want your best guys taking three-hour bus rides in spring training. This can lead to some weak spring lineups and disappointment for neophyte fans, who think they're going to see all the best players at every spring game.

Spring training in Arizona is where the visitors almost never take batting practice at the site of the game. Cactus League camps are so close to one another, most teams hit in their own complex, then jump on the bus and go to the game.

Spring training is where college teams often get to play against big league teams. Roger Clemens hurled against Harvard in 1987. The Red Sox annually play Boston College to kick off their spring season. The Rockies play host to the University of Arizona. The Braves play Georgia at the Disney complex, and the University of Tampa goes against the Tampa Bay Devil Rays. When they trained in Miami, the Orioles always played Ron Fraser's University of Miami powerhouse. Snowballing Baltimore southpaw Ross Grimsley was mercilessly ribbed by his teammates after Fraser's Hurricanes routed him in a spring game. Today, the Marlins play at least once against the Hurricanes in March.

Spring training is where silly stories can become big news. In the spring of 1987, the Winter Haven police came into the Red Sox clubhouse to inform pitcher Oil Can Boyd of some video rentals that were overdue. Naturally, the local newspaper unearthed Oil Can's play list, and the titles were predictably ribald, including *Nudes in Limbo* and *Sex-Cetera*. Western Massachusetts statistical wizard Chuck Waseleski dubbed the event "the Can's Film Festival."

When the games start, everything changes. The days are a little bit longer, and players hang around the park until at least two or three o'clock in the afternoon. The games are considered totally meaningless unless zealous baseball writers start to wonder if the team's losing ways might become a habit. Weaver knew all the spring training tricks. If a young player got the attention of the writers and showed too much promise, he would play the kid until the numbers fell, then ship him to Rochester. The inimitable Weaver had an answer for every six-game

JUPITER, FLORIDA

spring losing streak. He would stand before the assembled media and ask, "Can't you guys see what we're trying to do out here?"

Spring training is all about routine. Former Tiger shortstop Alan Trammell, now a coach with the Padres, remembered, "This is my twenty-seventh spring training. My first twenty-four were in Lakeland, Florida. I'm an old school guy. Lakeland didn't bother me as much as other people. If you really wanted some action you could go to Tampa or Orlando, which is not that far. Basically it was the same routine. Ballpark in the morning. Stay late. Go home and get something to eat. Watch TV. Get up the next morning and do it again. It was that way for forty-five days. I'm very structured. The nightlife and going out and going to the dogtrack, that was never me."

Spring training broadcasts can be rough on the announcers. Late in the game, managers usually substitute freely, and it's normal to see a lot of number 77s and 88s in the seventh, eighth, and ninth innings. Veteran San Francisco Giants broadcaster Jon Miller worked with color analyst Mike Krukow, who was known to simply give up trying to keep track of the minor leaguers; more than once he simply said, "Les Johnson is at the plate." "One time he had Les Johnson flying to left field, where Les Johnson made the catch," said Miller. "Then the next batter flew out to center, and it was Les Johnson making the catch again."

My first spring training experience was in March of 1976, when my *Boston Globe* pal Kevin Dupont orchestrated a week-long junket designed to take three fresh college grads on a tour of Tampa, Winter Haven, Lakeland, and Fort Lauderdale. The buoyant Red Sox were coming off their 1975 march to the World Series, and it was a thrill to see the '76 Sox getting ready for what would surely be next in a line of championship seasons. This was the infancy of free agency, and on the flight south I remember reading an article about a monstrous trade between the Orioles and A's that involved Reggie Jackson, Ken Holtzman, Mike Torrez, and Don Baylor. Years later, Baylor would be traded for a minister, Mike Easler, on Good Friday. ("It wasn't a good Friday for me," remembered Baylor.)

Back in '76, my friends and I were twenty-two years old, planning on being big-time baseball writers. We landed in Tampa, and our first stay was at the Bay Harbor Inn (now the

TAMPA, FLORIDA

Radisson Bay Harbor Hotel), owned by Yankee boss Steinbrenner. The lounge was called the Yankee Trader. Too cool.

After that, it was a series of Days Inns and Red Roof Inns, except for those nights in Winter Haven when the late, great Ray Fitzgerald let a couple of us sleep on his floor at the Holiday Inn. I remember sitting with young *Globe* scribe Peter Gammons, watching a young Montreal outfielder named Gary Carter slam into a fence in Winter Haven. I remember going to a night game in Lakeland and watching the Tigers and Red Sox from the rooftop of Joker Marchant Stadium. And I remember getting free drinks from the real writers at the old people's lounge at Christy's Sundown Restaurant in Winter Haven. It was a wonderful introduction to spring training.

Two years later, I returned to Florida as a certified member of the Baseball Writers' Association of America, covering the Orioles for the *Baltimore Evening Sun*. The team's head-quarters was the Dupont Plaza in downtown Miami. Decidedly rundown, the Dupont catered to Miami's ever-growing Spanish-speaking community. ("English spoken here" was a storefront inducement to lure guys like me.) I remember bumping into Hall of Famer Frank Robinson, who annually put himself on a spring training diet. This particular year it was the Grapefruit Diet. "It's okay for the first few days," explained the fifth-greatest home run hitter of all time. "Then you get a little tired of grapefruit, and after about a week you want to find a grapefruit farmer and blow his fuckin' head off."

Oriole employees and Baltimore sportswriters rented cars from the local dealer, Jerry Selig, a brother of Brewer owner Bud Selig, who eventually became commissioner of baseball. Most of the players rented condos and apartments on nearby Key Biscayne, but it wasn't unusu-al for some "name" players to live at the team hotel, the Dupont Plaza.

Cal Ripken, Sr., Earl Weaver's third base coach, often invited young baseball writers to dinner at the Dupont's restaurant. Ambiance was lacking at the Dupont. Sometimes mice would scurry across the carpet while you were waiting for your main course. The Orioles had

FORT MYERS, FLORIDA

moved to the Dupont from the McAlister Hotel, where Weaver claimed to have had a room with no window. ("I had to call the front desk every day to find out what to wear," said Weaver.)

Earl loved to drink and tell stories, and he would occasionally make an appearance at the Dupont lounge. I remember one night when he marveled at the exploits of an Oriole catcher in West Palm Beach earlier that day. Dave Criscione was a backup backstop who stood 5-8 and played only seven games in his major league career. But against the Braves on this particular March afternoon in 1978, he'd caught three foul pop-ups in a single inning.

"That's a record," Earl correctly insisted. "You can tie that record, but you'll never see it beaten. I've never seen it in all my years in baseball."

Life at the team's hotel can be pretty cushy for players and writers. There's room service, maid service, and laundry service. Tim Kurkjian, now with ESPN, learned a valuable lesson in the spring of 1982, when he was sent to Pompano Beach, Florida, to cover the Rangers for the *Dallas Morning News*. Tim was only twenty-five years old and hadn't traveled much. He covered the Rangers doggedly for six weeks, never bothering to go to a Laundromat or send out his dirty stuff. The Rangers opened at Yankee Stadium that year, so Tim brought six weeks of dirty laundry to the New York Sheraton and decided to send it out for cleaning. When the kind bellhop asked, "Do you want this back today?" Tim said, "Sure, why not?" Four hours later, the bellhop arrived with dozens of pairs of socks on hangers, folded underwear, and the rest, and announced, "That'll be one seventy-eight." The innocent Kurkjian handed the man a five-dollar bill and said, "Keep the change," only to be told he owed $178. Kurkjian said, "Can't you just keep the clothes instead?"

The Montreal Expos, almost folded by Commissioner Bud Selig in the winter of 2001–2002, put players up at the Fairfield Inn in Jupiter in the spring of 2002. The hotel's director of sales, Amanda Nieman, sent a detailed letter to each ballplayer outlining the house rules, including, "If you take your pillow with you to the games make sure you bring them back, we are not giving out any extra pillows for lost ones. Do not write, draw or carve anything in the elevator or anywhere else in this hotel."

In the spring of 2002, I traveled to Florida and Arizona with a two-time Pulitzer Prize–winning photographer and best friend, Stan Grossfeld. Our tour of the two states covered much of Florida and all ten spring sites in Arizona. We put more than 1,500 miles on two rental cars and saw license plates from forty-seven states (missing only Vermont, Louisiana, and Hawaii). We never saw more happy people at baseball games.

We played basketball at night, sweating in Florida, gasping for air in Tucson. Our jealous families and friends embraced the mission and made us promise to take them next time. We spent three nights talking baseball and drinking margaritas at the Pink Pony in Scottsdale, Arizona, and smiled when we read the words of proprietor Charlie Briley:

"After Christmas, when I was a boy, I used to cry sometimes. My mother would ask me why, and I'd tell her, 'Because it's a whole year till next Christmas.' And that's how I feel about spring training. When it's over, I want to cry."

Sounds like the sentiments expressed by *San Francisco Chronicle* sportswriter Dave Bush, who spoke for all fans when he said, "It's a pity they have to ruin the baseball season by playing it."

CHAPTER ONE

PITCHERS AND CATCHERS
REPORT

BOSTON, MASSACHUSETTS, IN FEBRUARY

The truck. It's baseball's answer to Groundhog Day.

Starved fans, desperate for another hardball summer, wake up one morning in the second week of February, unfold the frost-covered morning paper, and see the cornball photograph of a moving van parked outside the local ballpark. The truck will carry bats, balls, helmets, jockstraps, and the hopes of every fan. Spring training is about to start. Pitchers and catchers report on February 16. Six more weeks of winter. But where the truck is going, there will be sunshine and green grass and hot nights and cold beer.

There is no shortage of baseball news between October and February, but most of it involves free agency, trades, arbitration cases, and those horrible labor issues. A free agent signing in November can generate as much fan excitement as a ten-game winning streak in July, but nothing warms the hearts of the true fans more than the prospect of another season. Certainly this is going to be "our year."

Bill Veeck called it "the true harbinger of spring, no crocuses or swallows returning to Capistrano, but the sound of the bat on the ball."

The truck carries more than baseball stuff and regional hope. It also holds playpens, tricycles, kiddie pools, and car seats—all the things the players need to take care of their families. In most cities, players are invited to leave their stuff at the ballpark. In this century, most married big league players set up house in three independent locations: the regular season, off-season, and spring season sites. Roger and Debbie Clemens and their four sons live in metropolitan New York during the Yankees' regular season, in Katy, Texas, during the winter, and in Tampa during the Yankee spring. Baseball wives enjoy the perks of wealth and fame, but it's a challenge to run households in three cities per year.

Left: The Philadelphia Phillies in St. Petersburg, Florida.
Below: The New York Yankees at spring training in 1924. Babe Ruth is in the center.

The truck is not a big deal in Tampa because the Devil Rays train only a few miles from their regular-season home. It's probably not much of a story in apathetic Montreal, either. But in a baseball-crazed region like New England, the truck photo is a tradition on a par with America watching the Detroit Lions play football on TV after Thanksgiving dinner. Boston radio stations have been known to monitor the progress of the truck, checking to see if it has yet reached South of the Border on its way from Boston to Fort Myers, on the Gulf Coast of Florida. But no matter where you are, the infamous equipment truck heading toward sunshine remains a symbol of baseball's start each year.

The origins of spring training are steeped in mystery, much like the debate about who invented baseball. It is known that in 1886 Cap Anson, manager of the Chicago White Stockings, took fourteen of his players to Hot Springs, Arkansas, for the purpose of drying out from a winter of booze-bingeing. But is that spring training or rehab? Two years later, the Washington, D.C., team went to Jacksonville for three weeks of preseason practice. This jaunt is believed to be the first Florida spring training for a big league ball club. Connie Mack was a little-known catcher on that team, and he later recalled, "By the time we arrived in Jacksonville, four of the fourteen players were reasonably sober, the rest were totally drunk. There was a fight every night, and the boys broke a lot of furniture. We played exhibitions during the day and drank most of the night."

In 1894 the Baltimore Orioles practiced for eight weeks in Macon, Georgia, under the tutelage of manager Ned Hanlon. The team included Wee Willie Keeler and John McGraw and went on to win the pennant. Those Orioles were masters of the hit-and-run plays they'd perfected in spring workouts, and McGraw went on to become the godfather of what we know today as spring training. Frankie Frisch, who played for McGraw in 1920, would later say, "Many modern training camps are little colleges of baseball knowledge. Mr. McGraw delivered no lectures . . . He had little formal education and saw no reason why a man should know more than how to play winning baseball. And to play winning baseball, a man had to hit his peak of physical perfection in the spring."

In 1907 McGraw took the Giants all the way across the country on a trip that served as the first of baseball's barnstorming tours. Most teams later stopped in towns for exhibitions as they made their way home from spring training, and to this day many clubs play one or two games in non–big league, non–spring training towns before Opening Day.

In the early years of the last century, the players almost always got to spring training by automobile or train, and the routine called for hitting and fielding practice in the morning and long hikes in the countryside in the afternoon. Wearing cleats, sweaters, and ball caps, the 1909 Red Sox hiked through the countryside when the team trained in Hot Springs, Arkansas. Imagine it today. Wouldn't it be great to see Dodgers Kevin Brown, Brian Jordan, and Shawn Green together, hiking on the golf courses of Vero Beach?

Al Lang was a pivotal character in the beginnings of Florida spring training. In 1911 he was a forty-something Pittsburgh businessman who fell ill and was told he had six months to live. He moved to St. Petersburg, recovered, became mayor, and talked the St. Louis Browns into training in his town in 1914. It was an easy sell, because the Browns and other teams were frustrated by a long stretch of inclement spring weather at training sites in Arkansas. The Browns' first game against the Cubs drew 4,000 fans. The site, which eventually became Al Lang Field, housed the

Ted Williams in
Scottsdale, Arizona

St. Louis Cardinals for half a century before the Cards moved to Jupiter, Florida. Al Lang Field, now the home of the Devil Rays, overlooks Tampa Bay and is one of the more picturesque Florida parks. Al Lang enjoyed spring training baseball here until the ripe old age of eighty-nine.

By 1923, seven major league teams held spring training in Florida. Mack took the Philadelphia Athletics to Fort Myers in 1925. Thomas Edison, who owned a house in Fort Myers, visited the team at Terry Park, played catch, and took a few swings. He also invited the players to his home and gave them cigars. Babe Ruth and the Yankees came through town on March 25 of that first Fort Myers spring. In 1925 the Yanks moved from New Orleans to St. Petersburg, and pinstripe folklore holds that the Yankees made the switch because the Bambino couldn't resist the temptations of the Big Easy.

In 1929 ten of sixteen big league teams trained in Florida. In 1936 twenty-one-year-old Joe DiMaggio got in a car in San Francisco with Yankees Frank Crosetti and Tony Lazzeri for the long drive to Miller Huggins Field in St. Petersburg. It was DiMaggio's first trip east of the Rocky Mountains. DiMaggio didn't have a driver's license, so Crosetti and Lazzeri never let him behind the wheel. Their backseat cargo generated a great deal of expectation, so they arrived at night, after the New York sportswriters had filed their stories.

World War II kept everybody home for a couple of years. The Dodgers went north to Bear Mountain; the Cubs settled for French Lick, Indiana, the birthplace of Larry Bird. During the war years of 1943–1945, seven teams trained in Indiana.

Dave Garcia, the former Rockies coach, who has been to spring training for sixty-five consecutive years, remembered training in North Dakota in 1941, when the temperature was only 13 degrees and players wore tennis shoes because spikes wouldn't break through the frozen soil. In 1942 the Dodgers trained in Havana, and Brooklyn pitcher Hugh Casey got into a fistfight with Ernest Hemingway after a night of drinking.

Bob Gibson, Al Jackson, and Curt
Flood at spring training, 1966

In 1947 the Giants and Indians became the first clubs to hold spring training in Arizona. Bill Veeck is the man most responsible for this move. One of the game's great innovators and promoters, Veeck—then owner of the Cleveland Indians—bought a ranch near Tucson after World War II. He believed the city would make a great spring training site, but it would be hard to commute to games in Florida. The Indians and Giants had been barnstorming rivals for more than a decade, and Veeck convinced his pal Giants owner Horace Stoneham to move his team to Phoenix for spring training. And so the Giants and Indians moved to Phoenix and Tucson respectively, thus christening the Cactus League.

The first days of spring training are the sweetest. It is before the games that the days are shortest and players spend afternoons fishing, golfing, and going to the beach with their families. Work generally takes place between the hours of ten and one. At the Kino sports complex in Tucson in the spring of 2002, World Series heroes Randy Johnson and Curt Schilling arrived for a routine late-February workout at 9:30 a.m. and were seen leaving the ballpark at 10:30. The following day's workout was "shortened" so the D-Backs could play a charity golf tournament.

The pregame season is filled with meetings and special events. Most clubhouses have sign-up sheets on the bulletin board, encouraging players to enlist in charity auctions or golf events. Teams often set aside a day for players to sign items. Major League Security makes the rounds and holds meetings with each team. There's an optional Sunday chapel service. The longest meeting for each team comes when Donald Fehr, the executive director of the Players Association, makes his stop in camp. The labor update can take two or three hours, pushing workouts deeper into the afternoon.

The games offer more action, but there's something special about the sleepy days before any semblance of competition appears. It's major league baseball in the purest sense, offering the best access and the least tension, and it's a season only true fans can appreciate.

Before any games are played at Hi Corbett Field in Tucson, the Rockies allow fans to shag balls with the players early in the spring. These official "shaggers" make arrangements to go to Tucson and help the Rockies prepare for the upcoming season. They get to wear Rockies shirts and occasionally receive a compliment from a big-leaguer when they make a nice catch.

In Peoria, Arizona, Mariner pitcher Shigetoshi Hasegawa, who played six seasons in Japan with Ichiro Suzuki, noted: "In Japan we don't play so many spring training games. It's just workout. For one month. Here there's two weeks of that PFP [pitchers' fielding practice] and catching ground balls and then games. In Japan, it's more exercise and fundamentals every day. Nine o'clock to four. Shagging. Ground balls. Running. People get tired, but we get a day off once every five days. Here, we don't have a day off. If they asked these players to do what we do in Japan, no chance."

Only hard-core hardball fanatics come to the minor league complexes for the pregame, still-life workouts of late February. Talking about the dead zone days of Florida, before the games, Hall of Famer Jim Palmer told the *Washington Post*'s Tom Boswell: "We'd give an autograph to anybody who was here today, but then, the people who are here today aren't the kind who would ask for an autograph. They're my idea of good baseball fans. Anybody who comes to watch you run wind sprints and play catch and cover first base on bunts is obviously here for the aesthetics. They have a feeling for the game. They're always good people to talk to."

These are the people content to watch the Yankees stretch in Tampa, to watch the Diamondbacks play pepper in Tucson, to watch the Dodgers work on pick-offs and covering first base at Vero Beach, to watch the Angels run sprints against the backdrop of the mountains in Tempe, to watch the Indians take batting practice in Winter Haven, to watch the Red Sox pitchers run their annual two-mile race—once won by Ramon Martinez and annually lost by Rich Garces. During the painful lockout of 1990, fans who must have been caught holding plane tickets came to Chain O' Lakes Park in Winter Haven (then the Red Sox, now the Indians) and watched sprinklers soak the perfect infield. Like Kevin Costner in *Field of Dreams*, they seemed able to see a game that others could not.

The Red Sox of the twenty-first century hold their pre-, preseason drills at their minor league complex at the far end of Edison Road in Fort Myers. Past miles of auto body shops, gun shops, pawn shops, and propane tanks, the complex sits at a dead end in the true sense of the word. There is no fan parking, so Sox watchers board yellow school buses from downtown and are shuttled to the site. Getting off the buses beyond the chain-link fences, they look like prison inmates sent to clean a highway on a work-release program.

The drills, particularly the ones before the exhibition games, are painfully tedious. Imagine watching pitchers work on covering first base on ground balls to the right side. Pickoff plays. Bunt plays. Cutoff plays. Outfielders taking fly balls off the bat. It's all part of the spring routine. Former Red Sox general manager Lou Gorman watched the drills and said, "We do that a thousand times down here and then still screw it up during the season."

When Boston's pitchers and catchers reported in 2002, interim manager Joe Kerrigan

Mickey Mantle and Roger Maris in Fort Lauderdale,
Florida, filming the 1962 movie Safe at Home

SPRING TRAINING

spent more than an hour on each of the first two days working on catchers "framing pitches." "I prefer to call it 'presentation,'" said Kerrigan. "We threw 23,000 pitches last year and three or four hundred of them could have been strikes instead of balls if we caught the ball properly and presented it right."

There was also plenty of PFP—pitchers' fielding practice. "I know the mundaneness of it, and you've got to make it interesting for them," said Kerrigan. "We try to invent different names. One year in Montreal we called it 'inter-diamond engineering.'" Some of the tedious inter-diamond engineering can be counterproductive. In 2002 Rockies coach Dave Garcia, a veteran of sixty-five spring trainings, recalled, "One year in Melbourne, Florida, I think we had eight boys that broke their legs in sliding drills." Almost at the same time Garcia was speaking, Diamondback third baseman Matt Williams broke his leg fielding grounders in Tucson.

Speaking of making things interesting, parking spaces can be coveted items at spring training. Back in the 1970s, outside Bobby Maduro Stadium in Miami, the Orioles posted nameplates for important personnel: "General Manager," "Manager," "Stadium Manager." They even allotted spaces to newspapers: *Baltimore News-American, Baltimore Sun, Baltimore Evening Sun, Cuban Star.* When he was a pitcher with the Orioles, Cuban native Mike Cuellar was known to park in the *Cuban Star* spot. "Cuban star, that's me," said Cuellar.

Lakeland was the site of a nasty parking story in 1981. Veteran Red Sox publicist Bill Crowley became annoyed when young slugger Jim Rice continued to park in the executive's parking spot at Chain O' Lakes Park. Crowley was not a young man at this point in his life, but as a veteran of a POW camp in World War II, he was not about to back down to a strong hitter from South Carolina. Crowley confronted Rice behind the batting cage before the Sox road game against the Tigers, and a scuffle ensued. Before it was over, Rice had ripped some skin from the hand of the elderly publicist, and photos of the confrontation appeared in the next day's Boston newspapers. Rice looked like the churlish star we've known ever since.

But such episodes are rare in the easy days before the spring games start. Rarely is there heard a discouraging word. The people who make the trek to watch spring practice are the ultimate, diehard fans. It's one thing to watch a meaningless exhibition game between the Giants and Cubs, quite another to find Hi Corbett Field in Tucson and watch the faceless Rockies practice rundown plays.

Sadly, this aspect of spring training has changed. Today there is no shelter from autograph toadies. Many of the fans who arrive in Florida and Arizona before the spring games bring items they want signed. And signing has become the bane of the players' existence. There is simply no way a ballplayer can win. Stand and sign for an hour, and you are still a slug if one person in the back of the pack leaves without a signature. The "no-win" aspect makes players more reluctant to start signing at all. The days of Palmer chatting amicably with a handful of fans at Bobby Maduro Stadium are over.

Part of the reason is that spring training has become much more fashionable in the last fifteen years. What was once the terrain of old folks (Vero Beach had Dodgertown, St. Pete was known as "codgertown") has yielded considerable turf to suburban families taking spring break on the coasts of Florida and in the deserts of Arizona. Word got out: spring training was

The Cleveland Indians in the lobby of their Daytona Beach hotel, 1952

cool. It was a way to connect with the unapproachable stars of summer. By the mid-'80s, even the tranquility of the Cubs camp in Mesa had been overrun with tourists and thrill-seekers. One reporter counted license plates from twenty-six different states in the parking lot. Security got tighter in both Florida and Arizona after the September 11 attacks of 2001. Fans were no longer able to bring coolers and containers into the park, and media members had their bags checked at the gates. In Mesa, the Cubs stopped allowing fans to bring bats and balls in for autographing. The Giants fenced off their parking lot in Scottsdale. The Dodgers stopped giving fans a free look at batting practice, part of a $50,000 security upgrade—one more introduction of harsh reality into what has always been the sport's most idyllic season. Even harsher: the Braves charged fans $9 just to watch workouts at Disney's $100 million, two-hundred-acre Wide World of Sports complex.

Charging money to watch workouts—weeks before games that don't even count— just doesn't seem right. It violates everything we've learned and loved about spring training. Fortunately, some of the best things about spring training will always be free, like the endless sunshine and the happy faces and that "got nowhere else to be, nothing else to do" mood. Says bestselling author Stephen King, "Spring training means the end of the winter, but it also means a lot of baseball people get together and actually have a chance to sit and talk." There's a wealth of downtime during those lazy days before the games, with plenty of time to reminisce. And if there's one thing we all know in baseball—talk is cheap.

CHAPTER TWO

THE GRAPEFRUIT LEAGUE

ST. PETERSBURG

A spring vacation in Florida is part of the American Dream. Families go to Florida to be near Mickey Mouse. College boys go to be near college girls. And baseball fans go for the sounds, sights, and *warmth* of major league baseball in February and March. Remember Connie Francis singing "Where the Boys Are"? Spring training is where the boys of summer are.

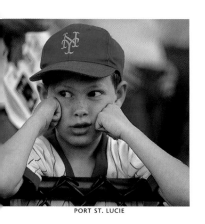

PORT ST. LUCIE

Americans have always had a fascination with Florida. To folks who've never visited, the image of the Sunshine State is one of a tanned George Hamilton, endless warm beaches, tropical drinks, and sunsets over the water on the Gulf Coast. In reality, most of Florida is blighted by fast-food emporiums, pawn shops, strip malls, strip joints, and thousands of miles of small, dreary roads leading past endless citrus groves and little pink houses. On the golden coast, wealthy folks drink gin on their beach balconies, but Florida's great middle is filled with Wal-Marts, Winn Dixies, NASCAR fans, gun shops, and—between mid-February and April Fool's Day—eighteen major league baseball teams.

Travel agents want us to think of silver sands and surf, but spring baseball fans are more likely to spend time on Route 60 passing through Yeehaw Junction or Alligator Alley, which connects the teams in the east with those in the west. Pick up your rental at Avis, grab a map, and check out the Indians by the banks of Lake Lulu. Or catch the Astros in Kissimmee (a perfect couplet for junior high humor—the Kiss-i-me Ass-tros). Meanwhile, the Red Sox and Twins can be found in Fort Myers, where the alligator-filled Caloosahatchee River cuts through a town that once protected new Americans from the Seminole Indians.

Most traditional major league teams train in Florida. The Yankees are in Tampa, the Tigers in Lakeland, the Indians in Winter Haven, the Phillies in Clearwater, the Cardinals in Jupiter, the Pirates in Bradenton, the Reds in Sarasota. The Dodgers—still a Northeast stronghold dating back to their Brooklyn days—

TAMPA

are in Vero Beach, perhaps the most perfect and pastoral of spring training sites.

All of the above are teams that "travel" well. These teams have longtime core constituents who like to make a pilgrimage to Florida to expedite the passing of another northeastern winter. Contrast them with a team like the Astros. The 'Stros train in Kissimmee, which is near Orlando, but they have no die-hard fan base, and what's the point of fleeing warm Houston in March for the sunshine of landlocked Kissimmee? The Cardinals, Tigers, Red Sox, Yankees, and Phillies have the ideal spring formula: a strong fan base in a cold climate with a team training in sunny Florida. Some of these fans wind up buying timeshares and retiring to the site of their team's spring training town. According to the Florida Sports Foundation, snowbirds bring half a billion dollars, providing 11,000 jobs and $75 million in salaries, to the Sunshine State during the six weeks of spring training.

Arizona boasts dry air, cloudless skies, and no rain, but many baseball folk still prefer Florida. Cubs general manager Andy MacPhail, who watches his team train in Mesa, Arizona, remembers Yankee spring trainings in Miami and Fort Lauderdale when he was a young boy and his father was general manager of the Bronx Bombers. "In Florida you get a better read on your players," said MacPhail. "You don't have the high sky and the hard infields that you have in Arizona. The ball doesn't carry as well. Sometimes in Arizona you get a little bit of a deceptive read." Eighty-two-year-old Red Sox instructor Johnny Pesky, enjoying one of his sixty spring trainings in 2002, said, "Down here you can perspire. I think you actually get in better shape here. I don't mean to take a knock on Arizona, but here you sweat, and I never heard anybody complaining about it. I think you could lose weight quicker here. I've seen guys come to camp in Florida twenty-five pounds overweight. They'd get that rubber shirt on and run around and the water would just pour off 'em."

Seattle manager Lou Piniella, who hails from Tampa, has trained teams in Arizona for the last decade, but he said, "I prefer Florida. I think it's easier to evaluate pitching in Florida than in Arizona because the curve ball breaks better." Piniella trained in Florida for most of his career

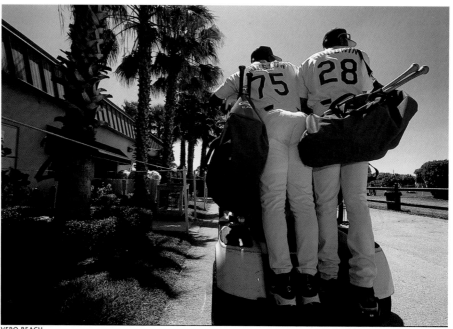

VERO BEACH

and recalls longingly the fun and sun of those golden days with the Yankees in Fort Lauderdale.

Today Yankees work at Legends Field in Tampa, the home of owner George Steinbrenner. They don't call it Legends Field for nothing. Whitey Ford, Yogi Berra, Don Mattingly, and other living gods of Yankee lore who carry history in their golden spikes serve as special spring coaches. Every game at Legends is a sellout—not necessarily a good thing for those who remember the more spontaneous springs of years past.

Dedicated in March 1996, Tampa's $30 million, 31-acre mini–Yankee Stadium is nothing like the ramshackle spring ballparks of an earlier era. There's a monument park outside the stadium, with histories of all the Yankees who've had their numbers retired. There's a replica of the famed Yankee Stadium facade. The outfield dimensions replicate those of Yankee Stadium. The home team clubhouse is easily double the size of the home clubhouse at Boston's Fenway Park. Painted on the wall of the corridor outside the Yankee spring clubhouse is: "I thank the good Lord for making me a Yankee."—Joe DiMaggio and "There is no substitute for victory."—General Douglas MacArthur.

The Radisson Bay Harbor Hotel, also owned by Steinbrenner, is the Yankees official headquarters. The old Yankee Trader bar has been renamed "Damon's Grill," and there's plenty of signed Yankee memorabilia on the barroom walls. The bellhops wear Yankee garb, there's a Yankee Clipper function room on the first floor, and you can order a Bronx Bomber Breakfast Special for $4.49.

Not every team's site is steeped in tradition. Take the Florida Marlins, for example. The Marlins leave Miami's Joe Robbie Stadium and hold spring training in Viera to the north. Imagine. Going *north* for spring training.

The Tampa Bay Devil Rays, another team with virtually no fan nucleus, travel less than five miles to spring training. They leave the ugly, climate-controlled Tropicana D or dome for picturesque Al Lang Field in nearby St. Pete.

Al Lang was once the mayor of St. Petersburg, the sleepy town that was the original

FORT MYERS

punchline to "God's waiting room." Spring baseball has been played here along Beach Drive since 1922. One of the great moments at Al Lang came in 1987, when Red Sox starter Al Nipper almost started a brawl, hitting Met Darryl Strawberry with a pitch. It was retaliation for the homer Strawberry hit off Nipper in the seventh game of the 1986 World Series.

The most attractive feature of Al Lang Field is its location. Fans sitting under the concrete roof can see sail masts bobbing in Tampa Bay.

The Devil Rays have cut holes in the cloth that covers the chain-link fence on the first base side, and a sign reads, "Ray's Knot Hole Gang." There are green embankments in foul territory down both foul lines, and the giant St. Petersburg Hilton fills the horizon on the other side of 1st Street. The Hilton houses Devil Ray players and staff, and you get a good view of the ballpark from its Bay View Meeting Room. From the roof one can see Tropicana Field and Al Lang Field, officially named Florida Power Park. A massive power plant looms beyond the center field fence, negating some of the charm of the bay beyond left field. Fans at Al Lang can purchase Devils regular-season tickets at the same box office.

St. Petersburg's Miller Huggins Field housed the Yankees and the (original) Mets for many years. *New York Daily News* reporter Bill Madden remembered an Australian press steward at Miller Huggins who got annoyed when the veteran reporter Jack Lang consistently took a bunch of bananas home each day. "Lang, have you got a chimpanzee in your hotel room?" the steward asked.

"From 1947 to '61 we were in St. Pete at Miller Huggins, and the old clubhouse is still there," said Yogi Berra. "We only had one field. We'd have two workouts a day. In '47 we went to Puerto Rico, Cuba, Venezuela, and back to St. Petersburg. I had been called up in the last two weeks of 1946 and I thought I had a pretty good chance. The older players treated me real good. Charlie Keller, Tommy Henrich, Joe DiMaggio. Bucky Harris was our manager, and at the end of spring training they let you know that you didn't get cut. We opened at Washington, and I got four hits that day and played right field."

Head south from St. Pete and you'll hit McKechnie Field in Bradenton, spring home of the Pittsburgh Pirates. The Braves trained here when Yogi was with the Yankees. It's one of the last of the oldies, still rickety and lacking the standard amenities that have made too many of the new facilities indistinguishable from one another.

Team relocation has been toughest on Florida's southernmost counties. In the early 1980s, there were still five teams training between West Palm Beach and Miami. In 2002 the Orioles were the only big league team training below Jupiter, which is north of West Palm. And the O's were hoping to escape.

It's nothing like the 1970s, when the Orioles were in Miami, the Rangers in Pompano, the Yankees in Lauderdale (where they stayed at the Yankee Clipper Hotel), and the Braves and Expos in West Palm Beach. The Orioles were one of the first to bolt the region; a contributing factor was Miami's crime rate. The O's didn't have much space at Bobby Maduro Stadium (since torn down), but they might have stayed longer if not for fearing for their safety. When longtime Oriole hurler Mike Flanagan went to work for the Blue Jays in Dunedin, Florida, and was asked what was most different about his new spring site, he replied, "No armed guards in the parking lot."

Miami had other problems when the Orioles trained there in the early 1960s. Former Baltimore general manager Frank Cashen remembered, "We stayed in the McAlister Hotel, and 1966 was the first year they allowed the black ballplayers to stay in the same hotel as the white ballplayers. And we had just gotten Frank Robinson. Before that, our black ballplayers stayed in a boarding house across town in Miami."

The Orioles were not alone. Jackie Robinson broke baseball's color barrier in 1947, and when the teams returned to spring training after World War II, many cities in Florida had laws prohibiting sporting events with teams of both black and white players. Many hotels and restaurants were segregated; in fact, the Lakeland Holiday Inn didn't take black Tiger players until 1962.

The late Joe Black, Robinson's teammate, remembered the conditions in Vero Beach that led to the creation of Dodgertown: "Even though I got there five years after Jackie had integrated baseball, segregation was at its height. You had signs for colored and white. When Jackie first signed, the Dodgers would go to towns to play exhibition games, and the sheriffs were locking the ballparks or telling them that if Jackie gets on the field, they're gonna arrest him because they don't have mixed leagues. That's why they developed Dodgertown —so they'd have their own training camp. When I was there, if you wanted to go to church, you went to a section of town where black people lived. That's where we had to go to restaurants and movies. We didn't go to Vero Beach proper because we couldn't go in the stores

or the restaurants, and so Dodgertown was our home. They had theaters and movies for us. They had a golf course. So in reality we only had to go in town for a haircut. There was nothing for the Dodgers to apologize for. That was the mores of our nation. Baseball couldn't do anything about that when it first started. That was the law of those states."

Appropriately enough, in the first inning of the first Dodger spring game on March 31, 1948, Jackie Robinson homered into what was then called "the Negro Section" in left field.

Hall of Fame manager Tommy Lasorda got to Vero the year after it was built and remembered, "When I was first at Vero, the black guys could go into town, but they couldn't play on the golf course. Mr. O'Malley found out about that and said, 'By golly, we'll build a golf course!' And that's what he did." There are, in fact, two golf courses: a nine-hole layout—Dodgertown Golf Club—and the eighteen-hole Dodgertown Pines Country Club.

Built on an abandoned World War II air base (the navy used the Vero airport to train combat pilots), no spring camp is more steeped in efficiency or friendliness than Dodgertown. It's the Disneyland of spring training—no small feat now that the Atlanta Braves play at Disney's Wide World of Sports in Kissimmee. Dodgertown is where you can see the regal Sandy Koufax, still looking fit and trim enough to win twenty, working with young Dodger pitchers, then hopping into his blue convertible and driving out Jackie Robinson Way. It's a massive theme park, where the sports scribes feast on unlimited jumbo shrimp. It's a land of golf carts whizzing along Campanella Drive, Sandy Koufax Lane, and Vin Scully Way. Everything is painted Dodger blue and white, and there are giant baseball globes on top of the lampposts.

The Dodgers play at 6,500-seat Holman Stadium, and their front office works in a 23,000-square-foot administration building, which opened in 1974. They have six practice fields, four pitching tunnels, and ten batting cages. A modern, ninety-unit housing facility, built in place of the old military barracks, houses young players and Dodger employees. There's a swimming pool, tennis courts ("no cleats allowed"), a volleyball court, jogging trail, basketball court,

VERO BEACH

game room, and movie theater. The stadium club lounge in the conference center has two pool tables and trays of poker chips. Underground wiring was installed to prevent unsightly poles and wires. There's even a bicycle rack outside the administrative offices.

No spring site has better fan access. The Dodgers and their opponents walk through the crowds to get to practice fields and Holman Stadium. The little ballpark is completely open—no cover for fans, no cover for the ballplayers. There are no dugouts—just benches. For years there was no outfield fence, but a small fence was constructed after Richie Allen crashed into a Royal Palm tree chasing a fly ball. All but one of the original Royal Palms fell victim to the Christmas freeze of 1989.

Now new trees are in place, but one fifty-year-old original Royal Palm stands proudly in right field, to the right of the scoreboard. The fans are so close, they can hear the umpires call. There are only eighteen rows of seats. The Dodgertown crowds always sing the anthem. It is baseball's happiest place on earth.

Lasorda: "I say this without reservation, Dodgertown is the greatest spring training complex in the world. All the players eat in the same dining room together. The major league players are down there and the minor league players. I managed the Dodgers for twenty years, and if I needed a player, I got him right there. So whenever we took extra players with us, they were right there for us to take. The youngsters sit right next to the major leaguers. They eat and they train with the major leaguers. That's what makes it special and unique. There's no other spring training complex where everybody is together, majors and minors.

"My first year was 1949, the year after it started. It was an old naval air base, and Mr. Rickey got it for a dollar a year. We slept in the barracks like the navy did, ate the same way. We did the same things you would do if you were in the navy. And a lot of those rooms didn't have heat in 'em and it got cold at night, goddammit. I used to sleep in my uniform a lot of times. They tore the barracks down and built beautiful rooms, and now it's like a motel."

Dodgertown was rebuilt in the 1970s and underwent a $1 million renovation in 1997. Since 1965, the Dodgers have purchased 450 acres from Vero Beach. The site has been used by professional and college football teams and several Japanese major league teams. The facility is

TAMPA

the summer home of the Gulf Coast League Dodgers and remains open year-round. The Dodgers have signed an agreement to stay in Vero Beach through 2020. The town claims the Dodgers bring $36 million to the community each spring, including 27 percent of all hotel occupancy during the six-week season.

There is nothing beachy or beautiful about the middle of Florida, where a couple of century-old American League teams train. The hamlets of Winter Haven (once occupied by the Red Sox, now the home of the Indians) and Lakeland (home of the Tigers) are a short distance from each other. Equidistant from both shores, these sleepy towns offer a Florida you won't see in the tourist brochures. The roads are lined with trailer parks, fruit stands, and burger joints (where even the fast food is slow). The trucks have gun racks, the women wear tattoos, the Elks Club is for whites only, and Winter Haven for years featured a drive-thru Taco Bell with the pick-up window on the passenger side. When the coffeehouse waitress tells you she's from "L.A.," she probably means Lake Alfred. For decades, the Red Sox and Tigers vied for the mythical Polk County Championship. The winner got to keep a coveted plastic trophy until the following spring. The *Boston Globe* and *Boston Herald* put newspaper boxes outside the ballpark in Winter

Haven, and the *Detroit News* and *Detroit Free Press* can be bought after the game outside Joker Marchant Stadium.

Marcus Thigpen Marchant was a recreation director in Lakeland who pushed to get the stadium built. The Tigers have been in Lakeland for sixty-four years, including thirty-five at Joker Marchant. The citizens of Lakeland throw a barbecue for the Tigers every year, and one restaurant installed a satellite dish so the locals can watch Tiger games at Comerica Park during the regular season. (The Indians moved into Winter Haven after the Red Sox left in 1993; Hurricane Andrew had destroyed the Tribe's camp in Homestead, near Miami.)

Both parks—Chain O' Lakes in Winter Haven and Joker Marchant in Lakeland—have open bullpens in the right field area, just outside the clubhouses (Marchant also has Lake Parker beyond the right field fence). In the middle and late innings of spring games, it's not unusual to see sportswriters hanging out in the pens, chatting with the ballplayers, taking notes for the next day's sports pages. When he was in his sixties and seventies, Ted Williams would sit in the right field bullpen at Winter Haven and comment about the Sox hitters. He hated Walter Hriniak's swing-down-and-let-go-of-the-bat-with-your-top-hand method and would spit on the ground when some of the Sox sluggers took their hacks. "Watching Dwight Evans swing like

SPRING TRAINING

that makes me want to puke," said Ted. This was the same area where the Boston scribes gathered in the spring of 1978, waiting to learn if the Sox had pulled off a trade for young Cleveland ace Dennis Eckersley. When word of a six-player megadeal was leaked to the dugout, Bill Lee ran toward the scribes in the right field pen and exclaimed, "Send lawyers, guns, and money! The shit has hit the fan!"

Winter Haven's Chain O' Lakes Park has osprey nests in the outfield light towers (though the orange grove beyond the right field fence yielded to condominiums during the Red Sox surge in popularity in the 1980s). Wayward alligators have been known to visit the players' parking lot. It was then, and probably is now, a town with almost zero nightlife. The center of Winter Haven's spring training universe is a stretch of three buildings on the main drag of U.S. Route 17, a half mile from the ballpark. The first building is Christy's Sundown restaurant, where patrons are greeted nightly by the amicable Nick Christy, and a giant photo of Nick's huge head adorns a wall in the waiting area in the front of the restaurant. The lounge at Christy's is dark and vast, featuring dancing nightly. It attracts an older crowd, and more than a few baseball lifers met their wives at Christy's. When trade rumors are rampant in late spring, Christy's is the place to get the inside scoop from thirsty members of the Tribe brain trust.

FORT MYERS

Christy's was also the site of a Wade Boggs Moment. In 1992, Boston's final spring training in Winter Haven, Boggs and his wife, Debbie, dined at Christy's, and somehow Wade fell from the family jeep when Debbie wheeled out of the parking lot. Wade wasn't seriously hurt, but the back wheel of the jeep ran over his elbow; the next day the batting champ showed off scars from the steel-belted radial and announced, "I'm the white Irving Fryar!"

Next to Christy's is the Holiday Inn, spring home of the Indians. In the days before the big contracts, many of the star players set up spring housing in the team's hotel. Former Red Sox reliever Bob Stanley took his wife and three kids to the Holiday Inn, and at night before dinner he would play ball in the quad with his son, Kyle. It was not unusual to hear Stanley warning his son not to make any diving catches because "we're going to dinner and you're wearing your good pants."

When the Red Sox played in Winter Haven, the Holiday Inn bar would rock on St. Patrick's Day, as hundreds of Boston Irish toasted one another deep into the night to the tunes of the Clancy Brothers. The third nightspot in this row was the lounge at the front of the Howard Johnson's motel. In the spring of 1986, Boggs and reliever Tim Lollar had personally engraved barstools in the establishment.

Boston Herald sportswriter Joe Gordon dubbed this troika of bars "the line of death."

SPRING TRAINING

A line in the sand in a town with no sand. Another beauty of spring training. There's a line of death in just about every podunk town in Florida and Arizona.

Jupiter, just north of West Palm Beach on the east coast, is the spring home of both the Cardinals and Expos. It's a good deal for the beleaguered Montreal franchise. The Expos averaged 4,500 fans per game at Roger Dean Stadium in the spring of 2001, only 7,300 in Montreal during the regular season. Roger Dean is the only shared facility in Florida, and Cardinals games generally draw about 2,000 more fans.

The stadium is the centerpiece of a 110-acre, twelve-diamond complex that opened in 1998 with Mark McGwire crashing a homer off the Expos in the inaugural game. Both teams are contracted at this site through 2018. The ballpark, with luxury suites and a party deck, sits next to a golf course and a sixteen-theater movieplex. The park is also the summer home of the Jupiter Hammerheads of the Florida State League.

No matter who's playing, Budweiser rules. In a sense the King of Beers owns the St. Louis team, as product is never far from the lips of Cardinal Nation. In 1987 the Mets moved to Port St. Lucie, a quiet town north of West Palm Beach, off Florida's ubiquitous Route 95. A local developer, Thomas J. White, first offered the new site to the Cincinnati Reds, but their owner, Marge Schott, instead took her team from Tampa to Plant City, on the west side of Florida. Legend holds that Schott was swayed by an elected official in Plant City who was the proud owner of a St. Bernard—Schott's favorite breed of dog. When the Reds declined, Nelson Doubleday took the Mets to Port St. Lucie. Mets co-owner Fred Wilpson told friends that the team moved from the west to the east coast to make it easier for Doubleday to see his grandchildren when they came down for spring break.

"When I first came and looked at the place, there was nothing here," said former Mets general manager Cashen. "It was just a big cattle ranch." It's the Mets' loss. Thomas J. White Stadium is a serviceable, if generic, spring ballpark. The Mets play to relatively sparse crowds (the park is designed to keep most of the fans in shade for the afternoon), and the only special aspect of the fifteen-year-old facility is a swamp stocked with alligators beyond right field. The public address announcer advises fans not to fetch baseballs from the swamp. Otherwise, it could be Anywhere, Florida, if not for the presence of big-headed Mister Met firing T-shirts into the crowd between innings. They even play Sinatra's "New York, New York"—ordinarily a Yankee staple—after the games.

Spring training in Florida is all about getting there. Arizona has the short commute, but the Grapefruit League is the circuit with the long bus rides. Players holler "gator on the right" to break up the boredom and get the attention of the rookies.

"The travel in Florida was tougher, but we didn't mind," recalled former Tiger Alan Trammell, who rode the buses in Lakeland for more than twenty years. "We'd get on a couple-hour bus ride to Bradenton or Vero. We used to bond a little bit more, because that's all we had. That's how guys can kid around and play cards, and that's how team chemistry is developed. The travel wasn't really that bad. We all bitched and moaned, but that's part of being a baseball player."

Part of spring training. In Florida. Where the boys of summer play during springtime.

VERO BEACH

SPRING TRAINING

CHAPTER THREE

THE CACTUS LEAGUE

TEMPE

Touch down at the Phoenix airport and you know you're not in Florida anymore. The sunshine may be equal, but the air is infinitely drier and the terrain far more beautiful. Mountains instead of swamps, coyotes instead of alligators, dry air instead of humidity. Indian jewelry instead of Disney trinkets.

Rust never creeps into the underbelly of cars in Phoenix and Tucson because there's little moisture in the air. This results in tens of thousands of dented, low-rider cars that would be in dumpsites if they'd been driven in Florida. The Cactus State can't compete with Florida when it comes to strip malls or strip clubs, but one link between the two is a highway landscape dotted by aptly named Cracker Barrel restaurants, in which most of the patrons appear to have answered a cast call for *The Lawrence Welk Show.*

Get your rent-a-car at the airport, and the exit road practically pours you into Tempe Diablo Stadium, where the Angels work out in their red jerseys. Built in 1993, it's a beautiful park, but there's not much history. The most infamous episodes at Tempe Diablo both hurt the Angels. In 1999, when star infielder Gary DiSarcinia was chopped in the arm by a fungo bat swung by coach Joggin' George Hendrick, DiSarcinia broke his arm and was never the same player. By 2002 he was in the Red Sox camp in Fort Myers, Florida, trying to make it in the minor league camp. That was also the year the Angels and Padres got into a bench-clearing brawl, and Anaheim's lefty starter Dennis Cook opened the season on the disabled list because of rib injuries suffered during the fight.

Tempe Diablo represents everything that has changed about the Cactus League ballparks in recent years. The creaky, wooden parks of the quiet desert villages have been replaced by a series of nifty 10,000- to 12,000-seat ballparks in the middle of multidiamond training complexes. Sometimes the games are sold out (particularly the Mariners, in Peoria), and the ball clubs market the spring season the same way they do in the regular season. Business is business.

But there's a still a lot that is good about spring training in the Cactus League. The modern parks have modern amenities, catering to every whim of the fan. Prices are still reasonable, and in most parks there's five-dollar lawn seating in the home run zone beyond the outfield fences.

In 2003 there will be twelve big league teams in Arizona, eighteen in Florida. The Rangers and Royals switched from Citrus to Cactus after the spring of 2002, moving into a $45 million, fourteen-field two-team complex in Surprise, near Phoenix. In Surprise, the players will get from the clubhouse to the stadium through a private tunnel, another setback in the quest for easy fan access in March.

Still, most players agree that Arizona is a better spring training state than Florida. You don't sweat as much, but it never rains and the trips are shorter. It's easier to get tickets, access to the players is better, and media contingents are smaller.

Perennial Cy Young winner Randy Johnson was in West Palm Beach with the Braves early in his career, but he worked out in Tucson as a member of the World Champion Diamondbacks. "I had about five spring trainings in Florida with the Expos, but I like Arizona better," said Johnson. "The weather is more conducive for pitchers and for hitters. You're gonna have drier weather. There's less rain and humidity that you have to deal with. It's really humid in Florida and it rains once a day, and you're not sure if you're going to get practice in or not. Here every day you wake up and it's nice."

Hall of Famer Frank Robinson added, "I enjoyed Florida when I was there, but I went out to Arizona as a manager and I liked that better. In Arizona, spring training camps were in small towns and you could get around easier. You can break a sweat, even though you don't keep a sweat long. The weather is more consistent. Plus, I think the ball travels farther out there."

Leaving the chaos and saturation coverage of Red Sox spring training and strolling into the quiet calm of Tempe Diablo, one can't help but be struck by the contrast. In late February of 2002, it was odd to walk into the Angels' press box and see only two lonely reporters. Cheryl Rosenberg of the *Orange County Register* said, "I don't mind being here instead of in Tampa with the Yankees, where there's a dozen guys trying to outlast one another so they don't miss the big story."

She's right. Spring training should not require the long media work hours that plague the regular season, but reporters from New York and Boston face the same vicious competition in March that they see in September. It's not supposed to be that way, and Arizona seems to be spared from the bloodthirsty throng.

Stick your head out the back side of the Tempe Diablo press box, and off in the distance you can see the giant roof of Bank One Ballpark in Phoenix, where the Diamondbacks won the 2001 World Series. It's a long way from February to October, but only a few miles separate the Angels' spring home from the D-Backs regular-season den. The Diamondbacks' version of "going south" to spring training is a hundred-mile commute from Phoenix to Tucson. Their spring home is actually cooler than their summer home, for Tucson gets some heat relief from the four mountain ranges that surround the town.

Next to the swank Buttes Hotel, Tempe Diablo is a beautiful setting, despite the

TEMPE

looming presence of I-10 beyond the right and center field walls. It seems appropriate that a team from California would play in the shadow of a highway. Beyond the left field fence there is a grassy knoll where fans picnic and sunbathe during the games. Occasionally the spectators are interrupted by a home run ball.

The Angels moved to Tempe from Mesa in 1993. The old-timers fondly remember when the team trained in Palm Springs in 1961–65 and 1980–81. Original Angel Jim Fregosi claims the Halos were required to ride their bikes from Gene Autry's Palm Springs hotel to their spring training site. (New York Giant Hal Chase fell off a bicycle and broke his leg at spring training in 1913.) Palm Springs is also where the Angels posed four former American League MVPs—Don Baylor, Fred Lynn, Reggie Jackson, and Rod Carew. From 1966 to 1979, the team trained in Holtville, California, sixty miles west of Yuma and ten miles east of El Centro. Tracy Ringolsby, who covered the Angels for the *Long Beach Independent Press Telegraph* in those days, remembers staying in El Centro, where the big night out was visiting the Autry Museum in nearby Brawley.

The Chicago Cubs came to Rendezvous Park in Mesa in 1952 (when Mesa had a pop-

ulation of 18,000) and have played in the Valley every spring since except for 1966, when they trained in Long Beach. The Cubs play their home games in HoHoKam Stadium in Mesa, which opened in 1997. The field was named for the late Dwight Patterson, who is considered the Father of the Cactus League. A Mesa benefactor, in 1970 Patterson built the Dobson Ranch Motel, which housed hundreds of ballplayers through the years. He was the one who lured the Cubs to Arizona when the Giants and Indians were the only two teams in the state. In 1997 it was estimated that Cactus League ball had poured more than $1 billion into the local economy, and Patterson is immortalized on the left field scoreboard at HoHoKam.

The HoHoKam were a Native American tribe that occupied the region for centuries. Its name means "those who are gone," and the HoHoKam are considered one of the world's most advanced civilizations of the first millennium.

Security is tighter here and access more limited. HoHoKam seats 12,575, and the Cubs have led the Cactus League in attendance for twenty straight seasons. Outside the park, manned rickshaws are available to take elderly fans to their cars. The public address system features Sinatra singing "My Kind of Town" as fans file out after the games.

Cubs manager Don Baylor, who played nineteen big league seasons, said, "I've done a lot of spring training in both states. In Florida you can come in ten pounds heavy and you can lose it. In Arizona you better come in close to your playing weight, because otherwise you're going to have to starve yourself to death to make weight. Plus, the proximity in Arizona is great. You don't have to drive a long ways. The traffic is murderous in both places, but they love to run red lights in Arizona."

Any discussion of spring training in the Valley must include the Pink Pony. Without question the most famous spring training watering hole in the United States, the Pony has been a home to baseball people for half a century. It's where Ty Cobb and Ted Williams used to hang out. It's where Ernie Banks, Mickey Mantle, Don Drysdale, and Willie Mays stopped by for dinner on their way to the Hall of Fame. It's where trades were hatched by top executives and where baseball scribes told stories long into the night.

Charlie Briley has owned the Pink Pony for more than fifty years, but he was ill in the spring of 2002, so his wife, Gwen, sat at the bar and talked of the golden nights in Scottsdale's baseball hub. Gwen is Charlie's second wife. His first wife died of cancer, and when Charlie met Gwen in 1972, he said that if she wanted to stay with him, she'd have to learn baseball and she'd have to learn how to drink. Gwen's kept her end of the deal. On both fronts.

After caring for Charlie at home, Gwen can be found on the same corner barstool every night after eight, dolled up with a Saratoga long dangling from her elegant fingers. She'll tell you about the time a flat-topped yokel named Mickey Mantle hit on her (and was rejected) when she was a young woman working at a convention in Texas. Years later, when Mickey was a Hall of Famer and a regular Pony drunk, she reminded him of the incident. Ever the romantic, the Mick said, "Oh yeah? Did we do anything?"

Briley left his native Kentucky for Scottsdale in 1936. It was supposed to be a two-week trip to visit his sister, but he never left. When he got out of the army, he went to work as a bartender at a Phoenix steakhouse. In 1949 he moved on to the Pink Pony (unfortunately, there's no great story about the bar's name), and a year later he bought the joint. Charlie had a strict rule: no horses inside the bar. Dizzy Dean was one of his first customers, and the two men talked baseball nonstop. They also went dove and quail hunting in the Arizona desert. Old Diz started to spread the word about the best bar in Scottsdale, and when teams started to come to the Valley for spring training, the legend of the Pink Pony was born.

In addition to Cobb and Williams, Rogers Hornsby, Jimmie Foxx, and Joe DiMaggio were regulars at the Pony. Jimy LeFebvre once performed the Heimlich maneuver on Clete Boyer. In the spring of 1973, Houston general manager Spec Richardson was trying to trade outfielder Jimmy Wynn to the Red Sox. Boston's GM Dick O'Connell rejected the offer, but a

Dodger scout overheard the conversation and went to a Pink Pony pay phone to call his boss. An hour later, Wynn was traded to the Dodgers, and they wound up going to the World Series that October. When Natalie Wood married Robert Wagner in 1957, their wedding dinner was held at the Pony. The late Bill Rigney held court nightly. National League president Chub Feeney once bought a round for the house on St. Patrick's Day. Angel owner Gene Autry would sit under the framed jersey of one of his players in the southeast corner of the restaurant. There are framed cartoons (done by Gwen and a onetime Disney artist, the late Don Barclay) of Pony regulars over the bar, fifty-four World Series bats, and baseball encyclopedias behind the bar to settle arguments.

SCOTTSDALE

In the new century, hardly any baseball people come to the Pony during spring training. Some scouts and club executives still come for dinner and drinks, but it's rare to see one of the players. Gwen blames it on the money the new owners have showered on the modern players. Today the place to go to watch players is Don and Charlie's, on Camelback Road in Scottsdale. Don't be surprised to see Hall of Famer Dave Winfield picking up some takeout at the front door.

Don and Charlie's is packed every night in March, but Oakland traveling secretary Mickey Morabito said, "I'm still a Pony guy. It's not what it was in terms of people going there, but it's still great. When I think of Don and Charlie's I think of the old Yogi Berra line—'Nobody goes there anymore. It's too crowded.'"

The Pony is only a short walk from Scottsdale Stadium, where the Giants play their home games. The Red Sox trained here in the early 1960s, but the Giants have been at the site since 1981, and the ballpark was rebuilt in the early 1990s. Like most of the other Valley parks, there's a banked lawn beyond the outfield fence. Another nice feature in Scottsdale is a series of misters, which are used to cool fans in the seats under the roof behind home plate.

The Oakland A's spring home is next door in Phoenix, where the daily high temperature in March is 74.5 degrees. The proximity is unbeatable. If they were all playing home games at the same time, it would be easy for a fan to see the A's, Cubs, Giants, and Angels in a single afternoon.

Since 1984 the A's have played in Phoenix Municipal Stadium, where middle-schoolers direct traffic in the parking lot and raise money for school field trips. Fans walk over a bridge to get from the parking lot to the ballpark. It's one of the older spring parks in the Valley, with an open-air press box and a short, concrete accordion roof that covers only a small portion of the stands. The Giants trained here for many years, bringing the initial light poles from the Polo Grounds. Phoenix Muni has none of the commercial feel of the newer parks. Fans who want the old-timey sleepy feel of the Cactus League should visit the spring home of the A's.

The 145-acre Peoria Sports Complex, which houses the Seattle Mariners and the San Diego Padres, is the most remote of the Valley sites. It's a half-hour drive from Scottsdale,

TEMPE

which serves as the unofficial hub of the Cactus League. In recent years, the Mariners have become the dominant team in the complex. They've emerged as more consistent winners than the Padres, and their constituency travels better. Leaving the Pacific Northwest for Arizona makes perfect sense.

While the Valley is a haven for the rain-soaked citizens of Seattle and Tacoma, why would fans leave San Diego to see the Padres train in a climate that is no better than San Diego in March? There's some symmetry in the fact that the Mariners and Padres share a spring facility. San Diego and Seattle were originally granted major league baseball franchises in the same year, 1969. The Seattle Pilots became the Milwaukee Brewers; then the Mariners were born as an American League franchise in 1977.

The Mariners-Padres stadium is similar to almost all of the newer parks in Arizona. There's a giant green wall in center field (to provide a good background for hitters) and a cozy bank of lawn for fans who want to get sun during the games. The most distinguishing landmark on the horizon is the La Quinta hotel, which rises from the parking lot beyond the left field fence, just a short walk from Krispy Kreme doughnuts. The other distinct element of the Mariners' spring is the massive presence of Japanese media on hand, to chronicle the deeds of American League MVP Ichiro Suzuki. When the Mariners are taking batting practice, the area behind the cage feels a little like Times Square—everywhere you look there are Japanese people toting cameras. Many of Ichiro's spring training games are televised live in Japan.

The Brewers are in their fifth season at Maryvale Park in West Phoenix. It's one of the uglier neighborhoods in the Valley, with a succession of fast-food joints and strip malls reminiscent of too many spring towns in Florida. But the Brewers don't draw like the Cubs, Giants, and Mariners, so there's easy access to the players, and it feels more like spring training before baseball's new era of March Madness. Not too many cheeseheads make the trek to Arizona, but Maryvale offers brats and Polish sausage for those who dare. Conveniently, the Brewers' minor league complex is next door.

In the Valley, proximity is key. Short trips every day. On our last day in the Cactus League, we saw Ichiro hit a leadoff triple against the Padres in Peoria, went to Maryvale and saw Colorado Rockie Todd Zeille homer against the Brewers, then moved on south to Tempe Diablo, where Oakland's Eric Chavez doubled home a run against the Angels. Anaheim's Benji Gil cracked a sixth-inning single to complete the tri-stadium cycle.

There's not a long history of spring training in southern Arizona. For almost half a century, the Indians were the sole baseball inhabitants, training here from 1947 until 1993, when they made a radical shift to the Red Sox former complex in Winter Haven, Florida. For all those years in Arizona, the Tribe had to make the trek up I-10 to find competition. When Cleveland left, the Colorado Rockies took over Hi Corbett Field. They had the town to themselves until 1998, when the Diamondbacks and Chicago White Sox moved into brand-new Tucson Electric Park at the Kino Sports Complex.

Kino is a two-team facility near the foot of the Santa Catalina Mountains. The White Sox have six practice fields, all on the site. The D-Backs have to take vans to some of their ancillary fields. The stadium (of gorgeous maroon blocks and sand-colored stucco) is next to the Davis-Monthan Air Force Base, and fans have a chance to glimpse a Stealth bomber if they

attend enough White Sox and Diamondback home games. President Bill Clinton once brought *Air Force One* to the base and spent a little time with the Diamondbacks. Fans also remember a pilot waving to them out of an inverted Blue Angel during a postgame flyover air show. Strictly spring fare.

The two-team complex isn't ideal. The White Sox and Diamondbacks have been known to battle over the use of the main stadium, and the Sox have a clear advantage in field access.

The other southern Arizona park, Hi Corbett Field, has been the home of the Colorado Rockies since the Indians bolted for Winter Haven. The Indians, born in 1902, were a wandering spring Tribe before they settled in Tucson. They first trained in New Orleans; San Antonio; Alexandria, Louisiana; Macon; Pensacola; Athens, Georgia; Dallas; Lakeland; Fort Myers; Lafayette, Indiana; and Clearwater before finding Hi Corbett, three miles from down-town Tucson.

Buddy Bell, manager of the Rockies in the spring of 2002 (he was fired in late April), remembered playing at Hi Corbett with the Indians back in the days when every road game was at least a hundred-mile trip north. "That was bad. And when you were a player in those days you never missed any trips, because we didn't have sixty or seventy players in spring training. But overall, I liked Arizona for spring training and I still do. The weather is a little better than Florida. It beats Pompano, where I was with the Rangers. There we had the wind and the tall grass, and we only had one and a half fields to work on."

TEMPE

Hi Corbett seats 9,577 fans and has a great hitting background (from the rooftop you can see the Rincon, Catalina, and Santa Rita Mountains). It's also next to a zoo, which somehow would be better suited to a camp that housed a George Steinbrenner team. The main field and the surrounding practice fields were laid out and maintained by the legendary Emil Bossard, perhaps the most famous diamond cutter of them all. Baseball has been played on the site for seven decades, and Hi Corbett was a co-star in the 1989 feature film *Major League*.

Standing on Emil Bossard Field in the Corbett complex, former Rockies coach Dave Garcia said, "Mr. Bossard built the fields here and the ones in Casa Grande, Arizona, and also the ones in Holtville, when the Angels trained there. When Cleveland was here, they had the four diamonds. The ballpark is exactly like it always was. Let me tell you. I was with a club that trained twenty years in Florida. But with the Padres, Giants, Milwaukee, and Cleveland, I've been coming to Arizona for forty-two years, and I like it a lot better than I do Florida. One time in Florida we lost eleven consecutive days because of rain. Here you know you're going to get in a day's work, and the traveling is easier."

It's hard to say good-bye to Arizona in March. A tour of all seven spring training sites explains why the Cactus League will grow from ten to twelve teams in 2003. The Arizona experience offers more of the relaxation and spontaneity that made spring training so great in the first place. The Cactus League has fewer sellouts, more fan access, older ballparks, less (try zero) rain, and shorter road trips. Flights into and out of Phoenix and Tucson are far less crowded. Arizona allows fans a more pure, less stressful spring baseball vacation. If it only had an ocean . . .

CHAPTER FOUR

ROAD TRIP

PEORIA, ARIZONA

Planes, trains, and subways are an integral part of major league baseball's regular season. Teams go from city to city in chartered aircraft, eating jumbo shrimp and drinking fine wine at 10,000 feet. Meanwhile, many fans ride the rails. Folks in New York take the 4 train, the D, or the 7 to watch the Yankees and Mets. In Boston it's the Green Line. Chicago has the El. Oakland and San Francisco fans ride BART. Everything is different in spring training. Big-league ball in March is where the rubber meets the road. Major league players return to their minor league roots (routes?) and travel by bus from Winter Haven to Vero Beach and from Scottsdale to Tucson. Fans raid the fleets of Hertz, Avis, Budget, and National and navigate the highways and back roads of Florida and Arizona. Getting there can be half the fun, especially while viewing the mountains of Arizona or the beaches of Florida.

Once fans arrive at the ballpark, so much of what is good doesn't even happen on the field. The sights, sounds, and smells of spring training ball are unique to the Cactus and Grapefruit Leagues. Touch the players. See them sweat. Hear them swear. It's all part of the spring training experience.

In these next pages, Stan Grossfeld takes you to spring training—on the field, in the dugout, in the clubhouse, in the parking lots, and in the hotels and apartments where the big-league players live and play for six weeks of each year. Sunshine, baseball, hot dogs, cold beer, pretty girls, five-dollar parking, volunteers, snow birds, easy autographs, and competition without pressure.

Spring training road trip. Get on the bus.

SPRING TRAINING

"Players are what you go to watch in the spring;

teams don't begin to emerge until summer."

—ROGER ANGELL

MESA, ARIZONA

MESA, ARIZONA

FORT MYERS, FLORIDA

MESA, ARIZONA

"Spring training means a lot of baseball people get together and actually have a chance to sit and talk . . . Everybody knows you by your first name at spring training."

—STEPHEN KING

DAVENPORT, FLORIDA

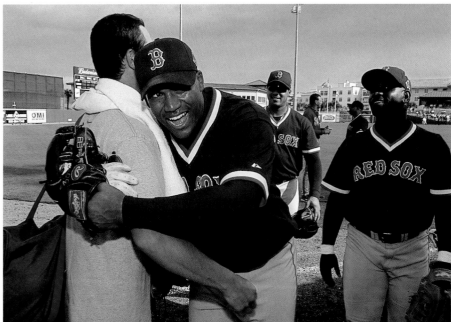

JUPITER, FLORIDA

TAMPA, FLORIDA

WINTER HAVEN, FLORIDA

"Can't you guys see what we're trying to do out here?"

—EARL WEAVER TO ASSEMBLED MEDIA AT SPRING TRAINING

SPRING TRAINING

SCOTTSDALE, ARIZONA

"Sometimes the more complex our society becomes,
the more people are reaching for what was once described
as a pastoral lawn game, which is what baseball is."

—ANDY MACPHAIL, GENERAL MANAGER, CHICAGO CUBS

TUCSON, ARIZONA

TUCSON, ARIZONA

SPRING TRAINING

ST. PETERSBURG, FLORIDA

FORT MYERS, FLORIDA

"There are wonderful individuals in this world who consider a baseball box score one of the four major food groups—something to be devoured over breakfast along with eggs, toast, and ham."

—DAN SHAUGHNESSY

FORT MYERS, FLORIDA

"I swing at more pitches in spring training. Sometimes you're hitting and you say, 'Man, I wish the season would start now because I'm hitting.' Then there are times when I'm glad it's six weeks because I can't hit to save my life."

—NOMAR GARCIAPARRA

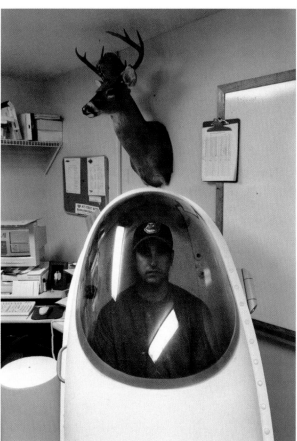

WINTER HAVEN, FLORIDA

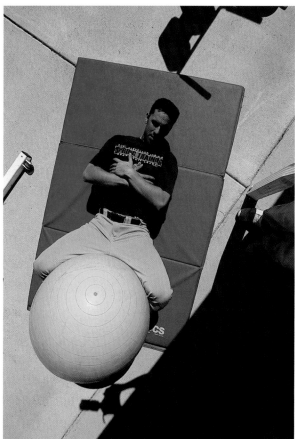

WINTER HAVEN, FLORIDA

KISSIMMEE, FLORIDA

SPRING TRAINING

TAMPA, FLORIDA

"Spring training is big-league ball without the moat."

—DAN SHAUGHNESSY

FORT MYERS, FLORIDA

SPRING TRAINING

CLEARWATER, FLORIDA

MESA, ARIZONA

SPRING TRAINING

ST. PETERSBURG, FLORIDA

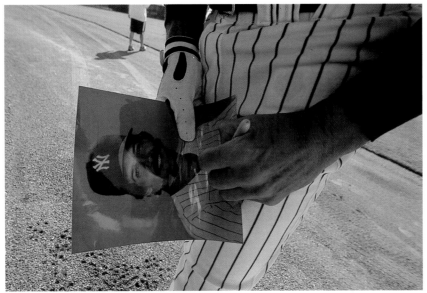

TAMPA, FLORIDA

BRADENTON, FLORIDA

TUCSON, ARIZONA

"If you really are a baseball fan you should go to the spring training camp of your favorite team, because that's where you get up close to the players. That's when they are more relaxed and interact with the fans a little bit more. It's just a fun time of year."

—FRANK ROBINSON

DAVENPORT, FLORIDA

PORT ST. LUCIE, FLORIDA

VERO BEACH, FLORIDA

SPRING TRAINING

FORT MYERS, FLORIDA

"A lot of California
girls came out.
They were even better
than the good-looking
women in Florida."
—Reggie Jackson

TAMPA, FLORIDA

SCOTTSDALE, ARIZONA

JUPITER, FLORIDA

TORII HUNTER, FORT MYERS, FLORIDA

"These guys today come here in shape. They're practically football players."

—GEORGE BRETT

SPRING TRAINING

BRADENTON, FLORIDA

WINTER HAVEN, FLORIDA

TUCSON, ARIZONA

　　　　SPRING TRAINING

BRADENTON, FLORIDA

MESA, ARIZONA

TUCSON, ARIZONA

JUPITER, FLORIDA

TEMPE, ARIZONA

CLEARWATER, FLORIDA

"The game has changed so dramatically in so many ways,

but not spring training. It's just the most wonderful time of the year."

—BUD SELIG

SPRING TRAINING

KISSIMMEE, FLORIDA

SPRING TRAINING

MESA, ARIZONA

KISSIMMEE, FLORIDA

FORT MYERS, FLORIDA

FORT MYERS, FLORIDA

BRADENTON, FLORIDA

LAKELAND, FLORIDA

"Temperature at game time, 84 degrees. Temperature in Minneapolis, 4 degrees!"

—BOB CASEY
PUBLIC ADDRESS ANNOUNCER AT LEE COUNTY STADIUM
IN FORT MYERS, SPRING HOME OF THE MINNESOTA TWINS

VERO BEACH, FLORIDA

Road Trip | 140

SPRING TRAINING

MESA, ARIZONA

"The girls are pretty and the sun's out and the grass is green
and it feels like real baseball, and at the same time
it's baseball with the pressure off."

—STEPHEN KING

TAMPA, FLORIDA

　　　SPRING TRAINING

VERO BEACH, FLORIDA (ALL)

"Dodgertown is the greatest spring training complex in the world."

—Tommy Lasorda

SPRING TRAINING

TAMPA, FLORIDA

JUPITER, FLORIDA

FORT MYERS, FLORIDA

FORT MYERS, FLORIDA

SPRING TRAINING

LAKELAND, FLORIDA

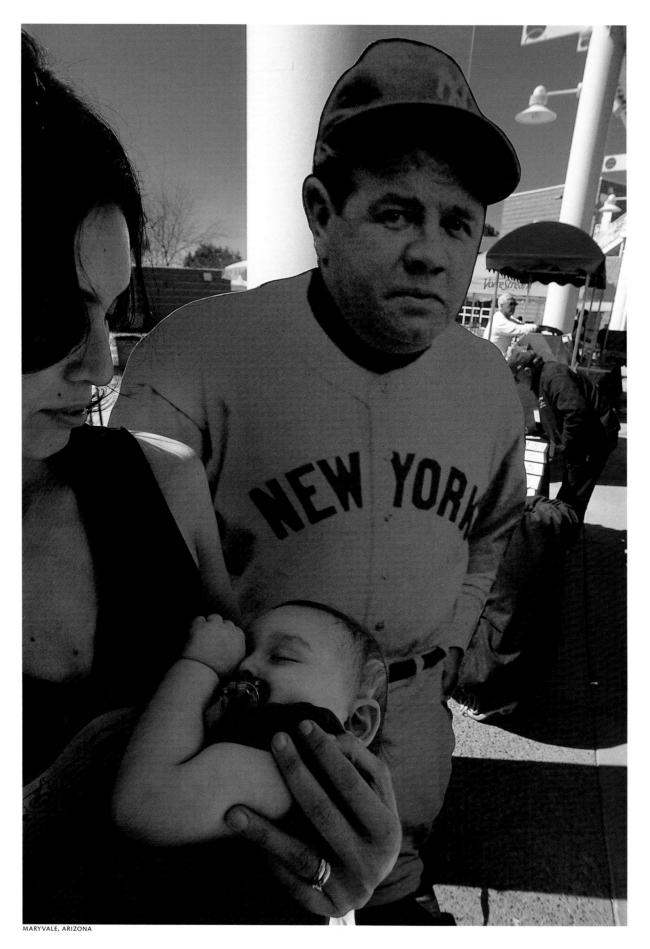

"It's okay to dream in February. Some teams are never as good
as they are before the games actually start."

—DAN SHAUGHNESSY

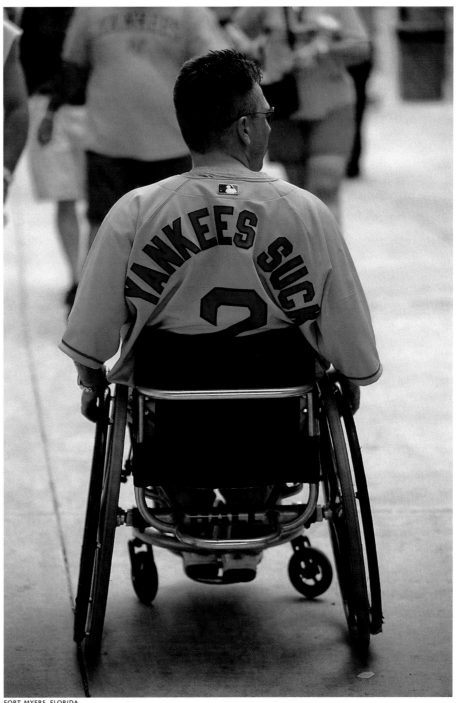

FORT MYERS, FLORIDA

SPRING TRAINING

LAKELAND, FLORIDA

BRADENTON, FLORIDA

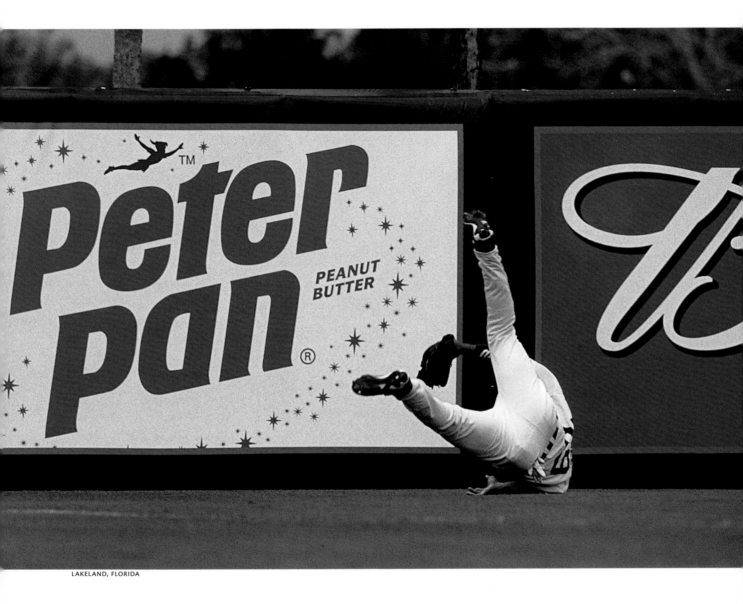

LAKELAND, FLORIDA

"The true harbinger of spring: no crocuses or swallows returning

to Capistrano, but the sound of the bat on the ball."

—BILL VEECK

VERO BEACH, FLORIDA

LAKELAND, FLORIDA

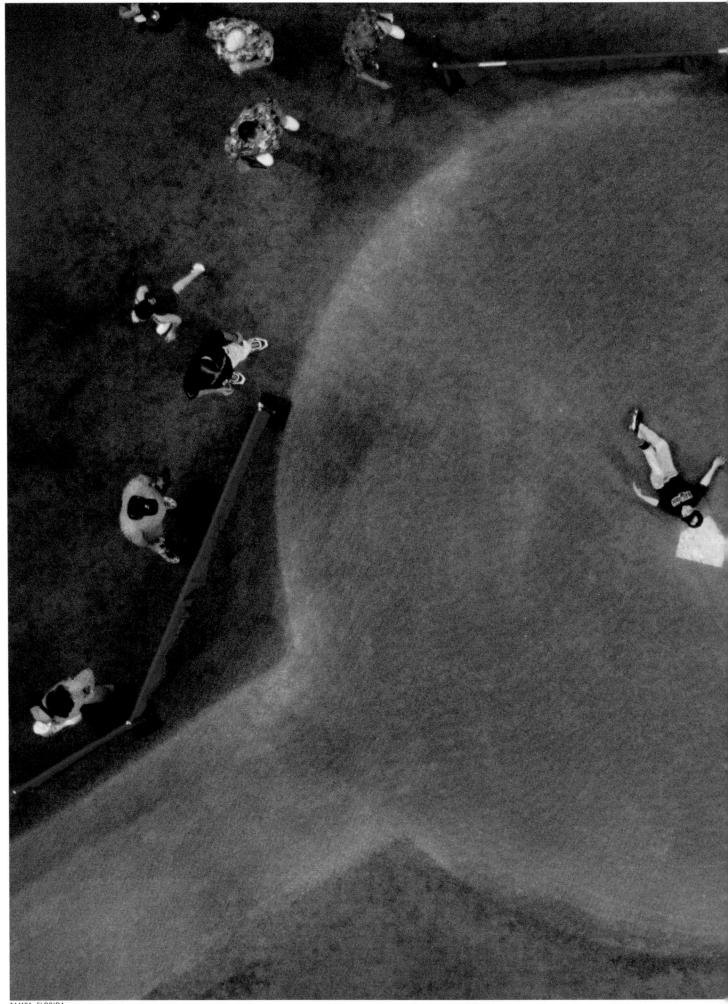

TAMPA, FLORIDA

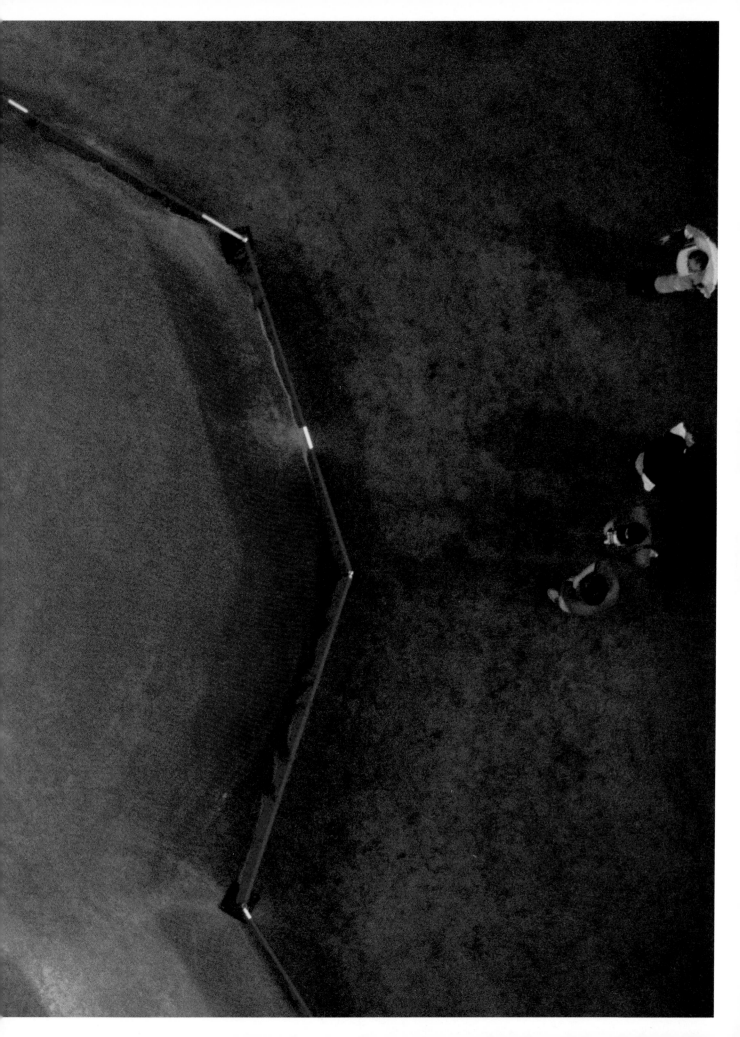

BRADENTON, FLORIDA

SCOTTSDALE, ARIZONA

KISSIMMEE, FLORIDA

SPRING TRAINING

FORT MYERS, FLORIDA

PORT ST. LUCIE, FLORIDA

SPRING TRAINING

TAMPA, FLORIDA

TAMPA, FLORIDA (ALL)

SPRING TRAINING

FORT MYERS, FLORIDA

SARASOTA, FLORIDA

SPRING TRAINING

"Spring training is the greatest excuse in the world to take a trip."

—ROGER ANGELL

CHAPTER FIVE

SPRING TRAINING
MEMORIES

Dom DiMaggio

A center fielder for the Boston Red Sox for eleven seasons, Dominic Paul DiMaggio was a perennial All Star and part of a .300 hitting outfield with Ted Williams.

I arrived in Sarasota in 1940 for my first spring training, and I had an inner confidence that I was going to be all right. Here I was, coming to the majors, and Joe had been such a tremendous ballplayer. I was known as his brother—a curious object then. If I tried to do everything at one time on the first day I arrived at spring training, I would be putting everything into it and leaving nothing else to be improved upon. So my strategy was to go slowly the first ten days. I'd take my five swings and swing very easily and hit line drives, placing the ball. Then I'd jog around the bases, and when I played in center field I did not go after every ball like I was playing in a game.

I recall very vividly our clubhouse boy, Johnny Orlando, who was a popular character, and he came to me and said, "Dom, are you feeling all right?" I said, I feel fine, why do you ask? He said, "It looks like you're not feeling too good, the way you are putting out." Then we played our first exhibition game in Tampa, Florida—of course, now I'm going to play baseball. Paul Derringer pitched and I got a couple of hits. At one point I was on second base and Johnny Peacock was on third, and my brother Vince was playing right field for the Cincinnati Reds. The next batter hit a line drive over the second baseman's head. I could see the ball was going to drop, but Peacock held at third, and by the time he got going, we were running neck and neck into home plate. And my brother Vince made a fabulous throw. In the process of trying to slide and then stopping I turned my ankle. So I was out a good deal of spring training after that. But I showed quite a lot in that one game and made the team and started the season in right field in Washington.

The younger guys were pretty much tuned at the start of spring training. When I got out of the service in 1946 we went to Havana, and you would have thought I never left the game. For me, I used spring training for getting accustomed to playing again. I always thought I was ready to go from day one. We'd play catch at the North Beach playground during the off-season.

"Driving across the United States is a long ordeal at any time, especially going diagonally from northern California to southern Florida, but if you think it's tiring now, you should have tried it then [in 1941]."

—DOM DIMAGGIO
IN *real grass, real heroes*

Doris Kearns Goodwin

Doris Kearns Goodwin is a Pulitzer Prize–winning historian and the author of Wait Till Next Year.

In the late 1970s, I was writing something for *The Real Paper* when I made my first trip to spring training. My son Richard was about twelve, and Michael and Joe were, I think, two and three. Even now, every time I go to the Tampa airport and take that shuttle bus, I can remember being there with the boys when they were so small.

We were in Winter Haven with the Red Sox, and I remember Richard hanging around those benches near the clubhouse and Jim Rice asked if he'd feed him baseballs while he took batting practice. It was really special. For a kid, it was a magical thing. Every day, that was his job, and when we were ready to leave Winter Haven, Richard cried.

My first encounter with Ted Williams also happened at that spring training. He worked with the Red Sox as a batting instructor, and I remember he was reading a book on Douglas MacArthur and Ted had been told I was a liberal. So he called over to me, "Hey, Pinko, I bet you hate this guy!" So I teased Ted that he reminded me of Lyndon Johnson as a larger than life character who never stopped talking. We talked politics for a bit, and it was great. That meant a lot.

It was the first time I had ever gone to spring training, and I was clearly a rookie. I loved the idea of that informality, the ritual of the day that mattered so much. Get up early in the morning and go over and hang around the place near the clubhouse and be with the guys and get friendly with them. I remember Peter Gammons so clearly. It was a sense of what baseball is in general, which is the ritual of the games and waking up in the morning and reading the paper. It's all deeper in spring training because your entire day has this schedule built into it and it's so much more relaxed. And for me, as a girl, it was fun to be in that environment because I had loved baseball for so long but never shared it with sports reporters. It was really fun.

Then I went back in 1979 to write an article for *Look* magazine. It was on George Scott, who was trying to make the team for the last time, and Joel Finch, who was trying to make it as a rookie pitcher. It was about the rookie challenge and the veteran challenge. It was my favorite in

some ways, because it was a character story of the two of them. Scott had lost a lot of weight over the winter. In Finch's first game, he was so nervous he gave up four home runs. He looked like the golden boy, and it all sort of went downhill from there. The funny thing about that one was that Don Zimmer's daughter was getting married and we all got invited, and it was at Busch Gardens. And I remember sitting next to Scott, and he had on this really fancy suit. And I said, "Boy, that's a nice suit." And he said, "I have a hundred of them. What you do expect me to do? Do you see me in Paris, spending my money?" It was such a great comment. But I got a chance to talk to both players at length about what it meant to make a comeback.

I think that was also the time that the ruling came down that said women could go in the locker room. So Haywood Sullivan told me, "Go in." What mattered to me was not seeing the guys in the locker room but seeing the difference in the quality of the minor league locker room vs. the major league locker room, so I could write that if Finch didn't make it. I actually went into the locker room when it was empty. So that big moment, the first woman in the Red Sox locker room, was not quite as dramatic as it might have been.

The last time I went there to write something was in 1986, when I went to Winter Haven to write an article about Wade Boggs for *People Magazine*. The article was basically about his sister, who had multiple sclerosis. She later came to Boston and I took her around to historic sights, and we got to know each other a little bit.

Everybody talks about the slow pace of baseball and what makes it so special and remembering all the things from the past. In spring training all that is exaggerated. It's even slower and more relaxed, and there's more time to talk, and there's fewer people there, and you really do feel that you are part of the whole process—watching the stretching, and then batting practice, and then seeing them play the games. Then you see them back at the hotel playing with their kids at the pool at the end of the day. It's a whole day's life of a baseball player that you don't get during the regular season.

George Brett

*A twelve-time All Star, George Brett played for the Kansas City Royals
for twenty-one seasons, his entire career. He was inducted into the Hall
of Fame in 1999.*

My first spring training was in Fort Myers, Florida. Terry
Park. I was number 76. It was 1972. Jamie Quirk and I
had been the top two picks the year before, so we both got
invited to big league spring training. We didn't get to play
much in the games. You'd never sniff the game field during
batting practice. We were always on field 2. And in those
days, we had only two fields. You'd go over there and do
your work with the coaches, then take the second infield.
But we had to make all the road trips and be lucky to get an
at-bat. They might stick us in there in the eighth or ninth
inning. I think I made it to the second cut that first year. But
it's always a good experience, even if you have no chance to
make the team, to come here and see what major league
baseball's about.

In '74 I almost made it. I was catching spring training
games as our third string catcher. They eventually sent me
down, but I was only nineteen years old, so it was pretty easy
to accept. They wanted me to play every day. Then, two
weeks into the '74 season, they traded Paul Schall and called
me up from triple-A.

When I became an established player, I didn't care
about the first three weeks of spring training. We had long
trips. Sometimes I'd take two pitches every at-bat, just to see
pitches. The worst thing you can do is sit on a bus for two
and a half hours and get up in the first at-bat and swing at
the first pitch and then get up a second time and swing at
the second pitch. Third at-bat. Third pitch. I hated that. You'd
be on the bus all day and you'd see six pitches. Spring training is about seeing pitches, working the count. So I'd take
pitches 'til I got two strikes, just to make sure everything was
there. If I struck out, I struck out. I knew I wasn't going to get
cut. If I had been fighting to make the team I would have
been more aggressive, but I was going out there just getting
ready for the last two weeks.

What's changed the most is the shape players are in
when they report. We used to come to spring training to get
in shape. We had one exercise bike. That was for guys with
bad hamstrings. We didn't have anything more than a three-

pound dumbbell in our locker room. I remember Richie
Hebner when he was with the Pirates, and he'd be wearing
vinyl pants and a vinyl jacket under his uniform in Bradenton,
Florida. Just to sweat it off. That's what guys did.

These guys today come here in shape. They're practically football players. They're on winter workout programs,
then they come here and there are workout rooms and
strength and conditioning coaches. There's just a lot more
individual work than there used to be—more coaches, more
players, more staff. There's so much one-on-one.
Everything's designed to make these guys better—and,
hopefully, baseball better.

Bud Selig

Bud Selig is the commissioner of Major League Baseball.

Spring training for me is like a rebirth. Generally, winter in
Milwaukee is long, depressing, and tedious. Spring training is our renaissance. You walk in to see the Cubs and Giants
in Mesa, and the sun is out and people are excited. It all
begins here. There's something wonderfully engaging about
spring training. Unless you've been here, it's hard to understand.

When I ran the Brewers, I always said spring training
was the nicest time of the year. The team was getting in
shape, hope springs eternal. It's the most relaxed atmosphere.
There are times I'm sorry when spring training ends, that's
how much I enjoy it. They play now in lovely ballparks. And
there is this wonderful, relaxed atmosphere, not to mention

the best synergy between fans and players you can find.

I've always been impressed by how many people go to spring training from places like Chicago and Boston. It's really remarkable. But then I realize that's how it all started for me. In 1957 I had just gotten out of the service and my parents were in Florida for a couple of weeks, and I said I wanted to see the Dodgers and Braves in a spring training game. In 1961 I went to Bradenton, Florida, with the Milwaukee Braves. I was twenty-six. I was a fan. I knew a lot of the players.

When we had our first Brewers club in 1970, we trained in a little facility in Tempe, Arizona. In 1973 we went to Sun City. I vividly remember 1974, when I was at spring training talking to our manager [Del Crandall] and general manager [Jim Wilson]. They said, "Well, I guess the kid will play short." And I said, "Who's gonna play short?" They said, "The kid. Robin Yount. Why not? He'll struggle a little, but he's ready." And they were right.

I had another spring training thrill in 1975, when Hank Aaron was with us. I came to spring training just to see Hank in a Brewers uniform. I'll never forget that first day I walked out and there was Hank out on the field. I thought, "The team that I'm president of has Hank Aaron on the field."

In the old days, the parks were sleepier and smaller. You didn't have the facilities you do now, and clubs didn't do much in the way of radio and television. Now it's become much more sophisticated. Still, it's not really profitable for clubs. You have a lot of players here and a lot of expense. I would say there may be a couple of situations where you make money, but if you break even, you're lucky.

Molly O'Neill

Molly O'Neill, food critic for the New York Times, *is the sister of former Yankee outfielder Paul O'Neill.*

Spring training was always a place where our family gathered. I have five younger brothers, and Paul, the ballplayer, is the youngest. Early in his career, we'd meet in various constellations when he was with the Reds. This was in the mid-1980s and the Reds were in Plant City, Florida. We loved Plant City. It's the winter strawberry capital of the United States, and for years we assumed it was named after strawberry plants. As Paul moved up and got more recognition, we were introduced to the mayor, and it turned out Plant City had been named after the local electric plant. But throughout that area, there were great roadside places where you would stop to get strawberry shortcake.

The games were much more intimate then. It was fun. Various brothers would show up, and my mother and father always went. I think everybody flew, although my parents might have driven from their home in Columbus, Ohio, the first couple of years. We would all just hang out at the games and catch up with one another. Usually there was some cheap motel where we all stayed. The first spring training we went to, we didn't know where to stay. It was Florida, so we stayed in some beach motel, but you had to go across two causeways to get to the ballpark. It took an hour. We learned that spring training is not really about the beach. Who cares about the beach? We would go to the beach, maybe one day, if the team was on the road. We would go to the beach once, and maybe Disney. But mostly it was about baseball. Eventually Paul rented a condo in an apartment complex and we commandeered the entire pool area.

I remember Paul's first spring training. It was his rookie year with the Reds, and there was an outside chance he could make the roster. I remember getting there the first day and there were all these baseball players on four diamonds. I ran to the top of a set of bleachers to try to find my brother. I remember the way I could find him: he'd always be the only one walking. Everybody else was running, running, running. Paul would be walking.

Then the games would start, and we'd all sit together and watch the players. We'd sit with my father, who had been a minor league player. My father and my brothers were really good at watching players and knowing who was who and what was going to happen and why. There would be family mood swings, depending on how Paul was playing. He would get off to slow starts a lot of years. So there would be these great bright suns and then these great dark clouds.

In one of the early years, my father took us to a Cuban restaurant in Tampa where he'd gone when he was a baseball player. We all sat and communed with his past, and we developed a taste for black bean soup. Black bean soup became very important. It was as if my brother was drinking the blood of heroes.

In spring training, we were revving up for real life. It was as if the other times of the year were hibernation, and now we've all sort of pulled ourselves out of caves and found each other and are getting ready for real life.

In the last few years we started enjoying it less and less. It got bigger. Stadiums got bigger. It got more like summer ball. Twenty-one years ago, you could still reach out and touch the players, and you did, and there was a back-and-forth and hanging out. There was a wonderful kind of chemistry between veterans and rookies—some would make it, some wouldn't. But as spring training got bigger, there were ushers and tickets, and the ballparks were more like junior stadiums of poured concrete. We were farther away from the field. It was more like a performance, and there was a kind of detachment that made it less fun. I didn't even go the last couple of years. I don't think any of us did. It just wasn't as much fun anymore.

Paul retired after the 2001 season, and I remember in the spring of 2002 I happened to call him on the day that pitchers and catchers reported. It was a really icky, cold day, and I asked him how he was doing. He said he'd been driving the kids to school and all, but he was feeling out of sorts. He said, "It's the first day. I'm supposed to be in Florida." I realized that's why I was sort of out of sorts, too. We did it for so many years, it became part of our biological clock.

Johnny Pesky

Johnny Pesky has served the Red Sox for sixty years in capacities ranging from player to manager to broadcaster to general goodwill ambassador.

I'd say I've experienced about sixty spring trainings. My first was in Rocky Mount, North Carolina, in 1940. My first big league camp was in 1942. The Red Sox player-manager Joe Cronin was ready to retire. He couldn't move, but he could still hit. Eddie Pellegrini and I fought for the job. At the end, I got to play against the Yankees, and I threw Joe DiMaggio out from the hole. They wound up sending Pellegrini to Louisville. But nobody said anything to me about making the club, not at first. We broke camp and went barnstorming and played games in Atlanta, Birmingham, Memphis, and Kentucky. Cronin still hadn't said anything. In the fifth inning of the game in Kentucky, I hit a triple off Johnny Vander Meer. At the end of the inning, Cronin came up to me and said, "Kid, you just made the ball club." I'll never forget that.

Back then, when we were going north, we slept on sleeper trains. Rookies slept in the upper bunks. Those were the loser berths. At the end of the day, I'd reach up and grab the bar and jump into my bed. One night Jimmie Foxx was walking by when I was getting into bed, and he put his hand behind my fanny and boosted me into the upper berth. Believe it or not, that was one of the highlights of my career because I'd read a lot about him and he was nearing the end. What a great guy.

We played more pepper in those days, and we didn't have as many players in camp, so you had plenty of time to get your work in. The spring games were different, too. You didn't play five or six innings and get out. You played nine. And we liked it because you'd see more pitchers. Ted Williams would gather us around and point out things about the pitchers, and it was helpful.

When I managed, we had nineteen-year-old Tony Conigliaro in Scottsdale in 1964. He had only played fifty games of minor league ball. I figured, he's here, so I might as well put him in a game. Our regular center fielder was hurting that year, and Tony hit the hell out of the ball in Arizona. He hit a ball in Scottsdale off Gary Bell that went over the center field fence by about forty feet. Of course, the air out there is much lighter, but it's still one of the longest balls I've seen. The GM wanted to send him out, but I knew we should keep him when I saw what he could do. So we did.

I still like to work out and hit fungoes in spring training. I get a little sore now and then, because I still think I'm twenty-five years old and I'm not. But that's what spring training does. It makes you believe you are young all over again.

Reggie Jackson

Reggie Jackson's career spanned twenty-one seasons, including eleven division winners, six pennant winners, and five World Champions. He was inducted into the Hall of Fame in 1993.

My first spring training was with the A's in Bradenton, Florida, in 1968, and I was nervous. The clubhouse was a rat trap. I didn't really want to go to the big leagues, I wanted to go to triple-A because I was a little afraid. But Bob Kennedy, the manager, said, "You're my right fielder and that's it."

I was ready physically when I got to spring training every year. I'd take a month off at the end of the season, then start working out after Thanksgiving. When I got to spring training, I just kind of got my arm in shape. I could have gotten ready in probably a week. I did the things I liked to do—shagging, throwing. I worked on hitting the cutoff, my fly ball, and ground ball work. All the fundamentals.

I took my time getting the bat ready. I took a lot of batting practice, which I enjoyed, working on situation hitting, 3-0 counts when we needed to hit the ball out of the park. Things like that.

I remember hitting eleven home runs in 1971 spring training in Arizona. It was a home run park, like today's big league ballparks. I was gonna set the world on fire, and then the season opened and I lost the bat I'd used all spring and I didn't get a base hit for a week. I didn't hit a home run for a month. From then on, I swore I would never hit more than three or four home runs in spring training.

When it came to Arizona or Florida, I didn't pay much attention to it. People said Arizona was drier and hotter and

you didn't sweat as much. What I noticed was in Arizona, I got to see Willie Mays and Billy Williams when I was a young player. I wanted to play against the stars.

My favorite spring training site was Palm Springs, when I was with the Angels. It was a small park and a lot of California girls came out, and they were even better than the good-looking women in Florida. That was a great, great place.

Spring training was always much more relaxed, especially if you were a star. I wasn't fighting for a job. I was there to get in shape and be ready when the bell rang. I was still hounded all the time, but in spring training there wasn't any pressure to perform. Your mind was down, so you weren't on edge. When the season started, I was on edge. People would say, "Be careful of Reggie and how you approach him." I was much easier to approach in spring training.

Arthur Richman

A baseball lifer, Arthur Richman currently serves as special adviser to New York Yankees owner George Steinbrenner.

I've been in and around baseball for sixty-five years. This is my thirteenth year with the Yankees, but I had twenty-five years with the Mets and eight or ten years with the St. Louis Browns, and I wrote baseball for the *New York Daily Mirror* for twenty years.

Spring training was always the best time of the year for me. It all started when I was at Brooklyn College and had a chance to go to spring training with the Browns. The college said I had to choose between books and baseball, and I

> "I loved Tampa because
> it had nice restaurants
> and a lot of dollies."
> —ARTHUR RICHMAN

chose baseball. So they threw me out of college, but forty years later, they put me in their athletic hall of fame.

I'd go with them to Burbank and San Bernardino, California. I served as traveling secretary of the B squad. I would write stories about rookies going to the Browns' farm clubs in Toledo and San Antonio.

When we were in Burbank, it was right across the street from Warner Brothers, and a lot of the dollies would come over and meet with the ballplayers, and all the guys would wind up with pretty good-looking women.

Coming back from spring training, we would live on the train and stop in little towns in Texas and Arizona. Rogers Hornsby was the Browns manager in 1952. We were in Texas one morning when he told me not to come to the ballpark with the team. He told me to stick around and bring Satchel Paige out because Paige was pitching and didn't have to be out for morning batting practice. I set it up with Satch. But when we got in the cab to go to the ballpark, the driver said, "Sorry, I don't take Negroes in my cab." Satchel went back to bed, and I took the cab to the ballpark and told Hornsby what happened. He said, "I don't give a goddamn if he had to walk, that's gonna cost him a hundred bucks!" Of course Bill Veeck, who was running the club, wouldn't take the hundred dollars. Hornsby had a three-year contract, but he lasted only three months.

Later, when I was writing for the *Mirror*, I'd go to Tampa for spring training. I stayed at the best hotel in Tampa at the time—the Tampa Terrace—which went for $4.50 a night. I liked it so much, I would go to Tampa every year on my vacation. In November of 1963, I suffered a ruptured appendix while I was there and I almost died. When I got out of the hospital after ten days, I saw a motorcade going by. There was no crowd. The man in the limousine stuck his head out, and it was President Kennedy. He wasn't very popular down there. This was right before he was shot in Dallas.

I was single until I was fifty-four years old, and I loved Tampa because it had nice restaurants and a lot of dollies. In those days, the players would all live in the team hotel. You would come down to the lobby and see them, and you might have a couple of toddies and go to dinner with them. Today you come down to the lobby and you might not see anyone you know.

Marty Springstead

Marty Springstead was an American League umpire for twenty years.

In the old days, they would assign two of us to one club, and wherever that club went, you went. Halfway through the spring, we'd switch from the Red Sox to the Tigers. Later in my career, they just started assigning us to specific areas.

For umpires, spring training is a time to get your timing back. Guys would work out during the winter, but you needed to work in the games again. It's a good time to work because the games go fast. There's no television, no time between innings, no pitch counts. You just go out and play.

One thing nobody likes in spring training is extra innings. I still remember a game in Sarasota when the game was all set to end because a runner was going to get thrown out at home plate. This guy was going to be out by forty feet. But stupid Ken Kaiser got in the way and the throw hit him in the head. The runner was safe, and we wound up going fifteen innings. Of course Kaiser stayed in the game. How could you hurt him? But I cursed him until doomsday.

I can't remember ejecting anyone in a spring training game—it's very hard to do. But it has happened. I remember Mark Johnson ejecting Gary DiSarcina in Arizona. Johnson had called out and their coach, Rod Carew, came out and said to give him a break because he was only a .240 hitter. Johnson said, "No, he's a .200 hitter." That really set him off. Goodnight, Irene.

Roger Angell

A longtime New Yorker *writer, Roger Angell is the acclaimed author of many books on baseball.*

I first went to spring training in the late '60s. Arizona. For me, I could do a lot of good work there, because I could really get to know the players. Their guard was down, and they felt good in the spring, and you could sit down and talk to them. You'd meet some legendary people like Hub Kittle, the great Cardinal scout. He'd talk about bygone players. It was the greatest excuse in the world to take a trip. And I was working.

I always connect spring training with friends. I've made a lot of friends in spring training, and we've had wonderful times. We felt younger. Whatever age we were, we felt young in spring training. There was so much fun. Getting up in the morning and going to morning batting practice or a B game. Everything is new. Baseball is new in the year, and there's a lot of young new players out there, and you turn around and there's nobody in the stands—basically nobody there. This is what life's all about. And I wasn't young back then. I was in my upper forties, but I sure felt young.

I loved driving from one camp to another. I would love to drive to see the Red Sox. To drive to Yeehaw Junction and make that slight turn to the right. It was a great moment in the morning.

Then there were people like Bill Rigney and Ron Fimrite, sitting around late at night talking baseball endlessly. Old baseball guys. It never stopped. Those were the days of the Pink Pony in Scottsdale. I remember Chub Feeney on St. Patrick's Day, having dinner with Bill Rigney and myself and a few others. And there was a notion that Chub didn't like to pick up the check. We outwaited him, and he lost his temper and shouted at us. And we said it wouldn't be St. Patrick's Day without some Mick losing his temper.

I can remember the great Oakland team of the '70s in Mesa, going into their clubhouse where they had their uniforms hanging from pipes, and Sal Bando saying, "Well, this is Charlie [Finley]. First class all the way."

I went to Vero to see the Dodgers a few times, and it was like a World's Fair exhibit. It was so planned. It was okay, but it seemed like premeditated charm, which has been the whole problem with spring training. It was natural before. In some of the places it was really a country fair atmosphere. But now the charm seems planned.

Florida got built up sooner than Arizona, I don't know why. Florida began to lose it and build bigger places. And everybody's heard about it now. When I first went to spring training, people were like, "What is that?" I would write about it. People would say, "Sometime we're gonna go." And they all came, by the bus-load, bringing their kids. And it was all gone.

The modern spring training ball-parks are like regular-season ballparks. They are all built up and they are con-crete, and the old feeling of spring training—when it was countrified and it was small and you could stand next to the players and the players weren't pissed off by the chain-link fences—that's gone. I remember Baseball City [Royals] when it was first built. They had security guards all over the place and walkie-talkies. This was spring training, and they are supposed to be letting you closer to the players. I went through the first time, and they passed me from one security guard to another. They finally stopped my car, and I came in and said, "I'm here to steal the bats."

Frank Robinson

Hall of Famer, former triple crown winner, and fifth leading home run hitter of all time, Frank Robinson was also the major league's first African American to become a field manager, in 1975.

My first spring training was with the Reds in Tampa in 1955. Tampa was fine for black folks as long as you stayed in the black area of town. It was tough. The only time you saw your teammates was at the ballpark. We stayed over in the black section of town in a private home.

But we only had to pay $30 a week for food and the Reds were paying $90 for meal money, so we'd pocket the difference. That was pretty good. We could come and go when we wanted to and had the run of the refrigerators, so we were actually a little upset when we were finally able to go down and live at the hotel.

I had a sore arm in '55 and I had no idea what I was

gonna be able to do. I didn't make it that year. I had a poor spring. But in '56 I tore it up pretty good all except for the throwing part. I hit well and played well, but I still couldn't throw early in camp. But Birdie Tebbetts had confidence in me and faith in me and put me on the team.

I used spring training to get in shape. We didn't have that stay-in-shape-year-round thing when I played. In those days, after the last day of the season you said, "It's time to relax now." And you would start to crank it back up and start running around the first of the year and then go to spring training to get in shape. I never had a weight problem, it was-n't that. It was just getting the reflexes back and getting sharp. That's what you used it for. Plus, spring training was longer then. There was more time before you started playing exhibition games, so you had a couple of weeks to get your-self ready.

As a manager, I don't like it because you get to the ball-park so early, and as I got older I found out you enjoy the game just as much but you don't like the early hours and the conditioning. And as a manager you have to worry about everybody. And you have to make some tough decisions, so it's not really fun. Let's say you have a young player that you invite to spring training and he got just four or five at-bats. He goes two for four and thinks he should make the club, and when it comes time to cut him, he'll be all upset. That's not a fun time of year. They don't understand, and most of the time it takes 'em a while to get over it.

Over the years I've seen better conditions, better fields, better facilities. Meal money went up. Hotels were better. Everything was just improved. I left a few homers there. One year with the Orioles, I had one hit for the spring, and everybody was worried. Then we opened up the season and I went four for five, with two home runs and two doubles.

I was always more relaxed in spring training. That's where the fans can get up close and personal. You're just out there getting yourself ready, and they are allowed to come down closer. That's a great time of year. I tell people now, if you really are a baseball fan you should go to the spring training camp of your favorite team, because that's where you get up close to the players. That's when they are more relaxed and interact with the fans a little bit more. It's just a fun time of year.

Stephen King

Stephen King is the bestselling author of more than fifty books and is a Red Sox season ticket holder.

Spring training means the end of the winter. That's great, but it also means a lot of baseball people get together and actually have a chance to sit and talk. This year I was able to sit for quite a while with two of the new Red Sox owners, John Henry and Les Otten. You go to Fort Myers and it's a real low-key atmosphere, and the games don't mean anything in the standings, and everybody's in a fairly good temper because they're glad to get back. The crowds are small; obviously the ballpark is a lot more state-of-the-art, for what it is, than Fenway Park is. There's only room for 6,000 or 7,000 people, but they always bang the place out and everybody is relaxed, and nobody is screaming or throwing beachballs on the field and no naked streakers or that sort of thing.

There are little rituals that are just great. The loudspeaker guy will come on in the sixth inning and say, "The temperature in Boston is 41 degrees and it's sleeting. And in Fort Myers it's 93 and sunny," and everybody cheers and claps. It's that kind of atmosphere. It's just laid back. You get a chance to talk to the players sometimes. In 2001 I parked and walked in past Jason Varitek, who was warming up, and he said, "Hey, Mr. King, how are you feeling?" And that meant

a lot. He knew who I was, but even more, he knew that I had been through a hard time. And he had a chance to say hi. The year before, I had sent Tim Wakefield a bouquet of flowers when he was supposed to start in Yankee Stadium. He remembered that and said "Hi" and thanked me, and I signed baseballs for them and they signed baseballs for me.

Everybody knows you by your first name at spring training. It's like a little town as opposed to a city. For me, it's a seventy-mile drive to Fort Myers. I've also been to the Twins complex in Fort Myers. I haven't even bothered to go next door to Sarasota, but I'd like to see the Pirates' old-fashioned, wooden structure in Bradenton. I probably will as the years go by. The first time I went was to a game in Winter Haven, but I don't remember anything about it. Those were my drinking days, and everything's kind of a fog to me. I know the spring training concession food is better and cheaper, and the beer guy can come right to your seat in the stands—not that it matters to me anymore, but Fenway doesn't have that.

I go down to the games as much as I can. I usually don't bother with the first two or three games of the year because they're so sloppy and everybody's just kind of feeling their way. I usually don't keep score. Sometimes I'll score part of a game, especially if Pedro Martinez is throwing. But I don't bother to score the whole thing because the players come and go and your scorecard ends up looking like a battle plan of the Romanian war. The crowd is different. It's an older crowd, a more mellow crowd. The people who show up at the bleachers in Fenway, we know they eat their own young. In Florida, fans are in their sixties and seventies, it seems. But it's great. The girls are pretty and the sun's out and the grass is green and it feels like real baseball, and at the same time it's baseball with the pressure off.

I'd like to do a book about the Red Sox after I retire. I'd like to take a year, from the beginning of spring training, and just sort of follow them for the whole year and write a book about it. And I think I could do that. It might be a little strange the first weeks, but you know what happens after that. If you don't shoot your mouth off and you're not publishing a column in the paper every three days, you fade into the woodwork, people don't even notice that you're there, and I bet it would be a really interesting book. I'd like to do that.

Grapefruit League

Florida

Atlanta Braves
Disney's Wide World of Sports
Baseball Stadium
Kissimmee

Baltimore Orioles
Fort Lauderdale Stadium
Fort Lauderdale

Boston Red Sox
City of Palms Park
Fort Myers

Cincinnati Reds
Ed Smith Stadium
Sarasota

Cleveland Indians
Chain of Lakes Park
Winter Haven

Detroit Tigers
Joker Marchant Stadium
Lakeland

Florida Marlins
Space Coast Stadium
Viera

Houston Astros
Osceola County Stadium
Kissimmee

Los Angeles Dodgers
Holman Stadium
Vero Beach

Minnesota Twins
Hammond Stadium
Ft. Myers

Montreal Expos
Roger Dean Stadium
Jupiter

New York Mets
Thomas J. White Stadium
Port St. Lucie

New York Yankees
Legends Field
Tampa

Philadelphia Phillies
Jack Russell Stadium
Clearwater

Pittsburgh Pirates
McKechnie Field
Bradenton

St. Louis Cardinals
Roger Dean Stadium
Jupiter

Tampa Bay Devil Rays
Florida Power Park
Home of Al Lang Field
St. Petersburg

Toronto Blue Jays
Dunedin Stadium at Grant Field
Dunedin

Cactus League

Arizona

Anaheim Angels
Tempe Diablo Stadium
Tempe

Arizona Diamondbacks
Tucson Electric Park
Tucson

Chicago Cubs
HoHoKam Stadium
Mesa

Chicago White Sox
Tucson Electric Park
Tucson

Colorado Rockies
Hi Corbett Field
Tucson

Kansas City Royals
Surprise Stadium
Surprise

Milwaukee Brewers
Maryvale Baseball Park
Phoenix

Oakland Athletics
Phoenix Municipal Stadium
Phoenix

San Diego Padres
Peoria Stadium
Peoria

San Francisco Giants
Scottsdale Stadium
Scottsdale

Seattle Mariners
Peoria Stadium
Peoria

Texas Rangers
Surprise Stadium
Surprise

ACKNOWLEDGMENTS

The authors wish to thank Phyllis Merhige, Ken Nigro, Ed Kleven, Kevin Shea, Kerri Walsh, Glenn Wilburn, Marty Baron, Johnny Pesky, Dick Bresciani, Mary Jane Ryan, Dr. Charles Steinberg, Rick Vaughn, Dan Casey, Bill Burdick, Rick Cerrone, Arthur Richman, Bud Selig, Kevin Dupont, Lesley Visser, Tim Kurkjian, Guy Spina, Bob Levin, Tommy McLaughlin, Joe Cochran, Pookie Jackson, Brian Mullen, Jack McCormick, Stephen Stills, Steve Sheppard, Paul and Marilee Comerford, John Maroon, Cal Ripken, Jr., John Iannacci, Rob Butcher, John Ioven, Catie Aldrich, Jim Wilson, the photography department of the *Boston Globe*, the Boston Globe Library, Maria Fitzsimons, Sean Mullin, John Horn, Jonny Miller, Mike McHugh, Sue and Dave Lodemore, Sue Callaghan, Jeff Idelson, Deborah Wrobleski, Rhonda Yakowitch, Mike LaVigne, Arthur D'Angelo and Sons, Glenn Miller, Bob Norcross, Jim Davis, Jim Mahoney, Frank O'Brien, Tom Mulvoy, Bill Tanton, Vince Doria, Don Skwar, Joe Sullivan, Wendy Strothman, Gary and Lynne Smith, Charlie Smith, Michael Sturgis, Vincent Musi, Callie Shell, Hunter Musi, Charley Kabat, Richard Serino, Wil Haygood, Tim Dwyer, Gordon Edes, Bob Hohler, Mike Barnicle, Dave O'Hara, Bob Lobel, Glenn Stout, Dick Johnson, the New England Sports Museum, Alan Waugh, Michele DaRosa, Diane Barros, Reid Laymance, Ken Fratus, Mike Openlander, Paul MacDonald, Ed Dicker, Ken Fischer, Steve Morse, Brad Canavan, Gracie Doyle, Becky Saikia-Wilson, Teri Kelly, Suzanne Cope, Jaquelin Pelzer, Karin Granga, the late Tom Winship, and the staff of the Pink Pony.

Special thanks to Harry Werlin of Calumet Photo, who has contributed to all seven books but was never acknowledged properly. You are the greatest. Likewise to designer Bill Marr at Open Books.

Thanks to the St. Petersburg Hilton and its general manager, William Giraldez. Also Spectrum Color Labs, Boston. Also Roger Berkowitz and Legal Seafoods.

Special thanks to Susan Canavan at Houghton Mifflin for doing the work and pouring the margaritas.

Bill, Lynne, and Dot opened their home to us in Arizona. Closer to Massachusetts, Dan had the assistance of Sarah, Kate, Sam, Marilou, and a raft of nephews and nieces anxious to contribute titles and ideas. Stan always had the support of Mildred, Sandy, and Angie Grossfeld and the home team of Stacey Kabat and Sam Grossfeld.

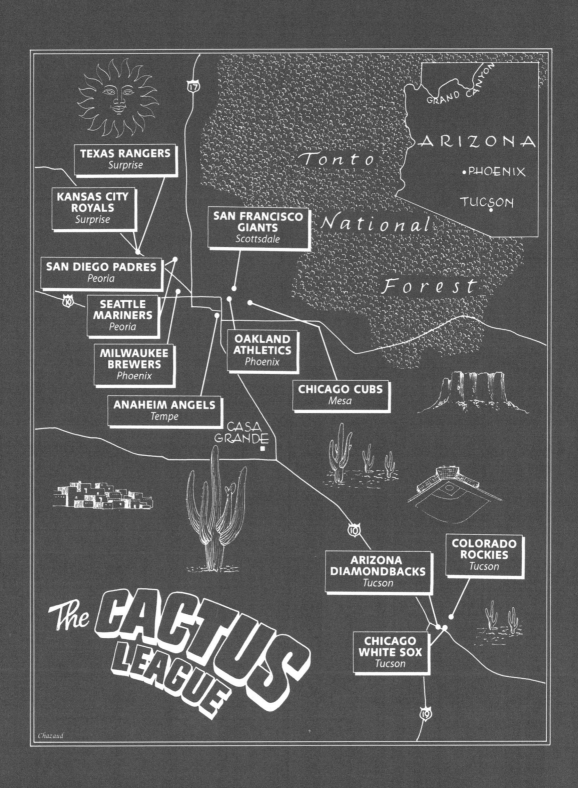